Speaking the Unspeakable

Speaking the Unspeakable

Religion, Misogyny,
and the Uncanny Mother
in Freud's Cultural Texts

Diane Jonte-Pace

UNIVERSITY OF CALIFORNIA PRESS

Berkeley   Los Angeles   London

University of California Press
Berkeley and Los Angeles, California

University of California Press, Ltd.
London, England

© 2001 by the Regents of the University of California

Library of Congress Cataloging-in-Publication Data

Jonte-Pace, Diane E. (Diane Elizabeth), 1951–.
 Speaking the unspeakable : religion, misogyny, and the uncanny
mother in Freud's cultural texts / by Diane Jonte-Pace.
   p.   cm.
 Includes bibliographical references and index.
  ISBN 0-520-22600-3 (alk. paper). — ISBN 0-520-23076-0 (pbk. :
alk. paper)
   1. Freud, Sigmund, 1856–1939 — Psychoanalysis and religion.
 2. Feminist psychology. I. Title.

BF175.4R44J66   2001
150.19'52 — dc21   2001027341

Manufactured in the United States of America
10 09 08 07 06 05 04 03 02 01
10 9 8 7 6 5 4 3 2 1

The paper used in this publication meets the minimum require-
ments of ANSI/NISO Z39.48-1992 (R 1997) (*Permanence of
Paper*).

To Amy, Clare, and David

CONTENTS

ACKNOWLEDGMENTS

I thank the many colleagues and friends who have read and commented on this project over the past several years. Peter Homans read earlier versions of chapters 3, 4, and 5. Jay Geller read chapters 3 and 4. Mary Ellen Ross and Marcia Mim read the introduction. Don Capps and Judith Van Herik read the entire manuscript. Marilyn Edelstein read chapter 2. The Person, Culture, and Religion Group invited me to present part of chapter 1 at the meeting of the American Academy of Religion in Boston in 1999. I am grateful to these readers and listeners for their encouragement and critical feedback.

I thank Santa Clara University for the sabbatical and research leave during the 1996–97 academic year and the spring quarter of 1999 that enabled me to write this book. The university also provided a Thomas Terry research grant which made it possible for me to hire three wonderful research assistants: Kathryn McNichols, Alicia Ross, and Charlotte Vallaeys. Vicky Gonzalez provided efficient and thorough administrative assistance whenever called upon.

I thank the *Journal of the American Academy of Religion* and Oxford University Press for permission to revise and reprint "At Home in the Uncanny: Freudian Representations of Death, Mothers, and the After-life," *Journal of the American Academy of Religion* 64 (1996): 61–88. I thank the editors of *Research in the Social Scientific Study of Religion* for permission to revise and reprint "Legitimation of Hatred or Inversion into Love: Religion in Kristeva's Re-Reading of Freud," *Research in the Social Scientific Study of Religion* 10 (1999): 17–35. I thank Palgrave Imprints for permission to revise and reprint "Turning Away at the Navel of the Dream: Religion and the Body of the Mother at the Beginning and End of Interpretation," from *Dream Reader: Religious, Cultural, and Psychological Dimensions of Dreams and Dreaming,* edited by Kelly Bulkeley, 2001.

Many others have helped give birth to this project. The students in my courses on religion in the theories of Freud and Jung at Santa Clara University have asked the questions that led to many of the discoveries in these pages. I thank my editor at the University of California Press, Reed Malcolm, for his patience and encouragement. Finally, I am most grateful to my family: Amy, Clare, and David Pace have supported this project with good humor for many years in spite of the "maternal absences" that went into making the book a reality.

Misogyny and Religion under Analysis

Masterplot and Counterthesis in Tension

Freud's Oedipal paradigm, characterized by death wishes for fathers and by erotic desires for mothers, constitutes what has been called his "masterplot" (Brooks 1989). It is the thesis for which he is best known and which he saw as his "immortal contribution" to Western culture (*SE* 5: 453). The Oedipal masterplot, articulated in Freud's earliest psychoanalytic writings and frequently reiterated during the forty years of his psychoanalytic career, provided the foundational structure for his analyses of psyche, culture, and religion.

Freud was deeply committed to pursuing and promoting the Oedipal thesis. Although he did not formalize it as a "complex" until 1910 (*SE* 11: 171), he described his earliest discovery of the Oedipal paradigm as a "revelation" (*SE* 1: 265), and he found Oedipal solutions to most of the riddles he encountered. But below the surface of this Oedipal masterplot, particularly in his writings on religion, lies another thesis, which might be called a "counterthesis." This counterthesis differs from the "pre-Oedipal" thesis evident in Freud's late texts and developed further in the work of object-relations theorists like D. W. Winnicott (1972).[1] It differs as well from the "anti-Oedipal" argument of Deleuze and Guattari (1983). Often interruptive and subversive, this counterthesis haunts Freud's writings as if to challenge the dominance of the Oedipal paradigm. It appears most frequently in images and metaphors which, although intended as support for the Oedipal masterplot, actually decenter it.

The Oedipal theory gives centrality to the father: the "father complex" is a term Freud often used as an abbreviation of sorts for the "Oedipus complex." In the Oedipus or father complex, death wishes, hostility, and parricidal fantasies are directed toward the father. Concomitantly, the mother is beloved: the mother-son relationship is "altogether the most perfect, the most free from ambivalence of all human relationships" (*SE* 22: 133), and the mother is the object of erotic, incestuous fantasies of sexual union. But there are exceptions to this pattern. On rare occasions, and with hesitation, Freud discusses death fantasies in relation to the mother, rather than the father, exploring matriphobic and misogynist fears and fantasies: fears of the mother, desires for her death, and fantasies of immortality. These Freudian explorations of matriphobia and matricide do not represent misogyny on Freud's part. Rather, they represent analyses and interpretations of psychological and cultural misogyny. The hesitant non-Oedipal speculations in which Freud analyzes death and the fantasy of immortality in association with the mother are part of what I call the counterthesis. They occur most visibly in Freud's writings on religion.

MISOGYNY AND RELIGION UNDER ANALYSIS

In this work, I expose the shadowy presence of this non-Oedipal counterthesis in the cultural texts on religion. My sources are not only Freud's four major "cultural texts," *Totem and Taboo, The Future of an Illusion, Civilization and its Discontents,* and *Moses and Monotheism,* but also some of his shorter writings related to religion and mythology ("Medusa's Head" and "The Theme of the Three Caskets," for example), and some of his writings which address religious themes and issues only indirectly (such as "Thoughts for the Times on War and Death" and *The Interpretation of Dreams*). All of these are "cultural texts" in a larger sense (Homans 1989: 196). They are not only about intrapsychic or interpersonal dynamics, but also about the intersections of body, psyche, and society. They address the sources and meanings of the fragile "achievements of our civilization" (*SE* 14: 307) embodied in art, literature, philosophy, ethics, religion, science, and education. Within these cultural texts, broadly defined, the counterthesis is apparent at several sites: it is particularly evident in Freud's writings on the maternal body, death and the afterlife, Judaism and anti-Semitism, and in his writings on mourning and melancholia.

Religion is not only the subject of the texts in which the counterthesis emerges most vividly, religion is also part of the counterthesis itself. Although it is never fully developed in Freud's writings, the counterthesis points toward a psychoanalytic theory of the loss of religion and the absence of God: it represents a step toward an analysis of religion in absentia, of Jewishness in the context of secularism, assimilation, and modernity. When one becomes attentive to the eruptions of this second thesis into the more immediately apparent Oedipal narrative, Freud's theory of religion emerges as a more complex theory and as a theory which points toward a feminist analysis of deeply rooted forms of cultural misogyny and xenophobia.

The counterthesis intrudes into Freud's texts in three ways. Some intrusions interrupt and subvert an Oedipal analysis. Others explicitly acknowledge the limitations of the Oedipal paradigm. Still others tentatively and hesitantly begin to develop non-Oedipal analyses. Although these three kinds of intrusion are sometimes overlapping, they can, at least heuristically, be differentiated.

In his first major work, *The Interpretation of Dreams,* discontinuities in an Oedipal argument reveal elements which have no place in the parricidal and incestuous paradigm. In the "dream book," Freud is quite cognizant of the limitations of the Oedipal theory. He discusses the point at which one must turn aside from dream interpretation, the "spot in every dream at which it is unplumbable, a navel as it were, that is its point of contact with the unknown" (*SE* 4: 111, n. 1). Freud's essay "A Religious Experience," written fairly late in his life, illustrates another sort of intrusion: non-Oedipal themes interrupt and subvert an Oedipal analysis almost against Freud's will. Still other texts, many of which date from the middle period of his psychoanalytic career, like "The Uncanny," "Mourning and Melancholia," and "On Transience," represent subversions of the Oedipal masterplot which enact explicit, yet hesitant explorations of the counterthesis.

The counterthesis within Freud's texts, a trajectory incompletely developed by Freud and virtually unnoticed by his previous interpreters, points suggestively toward new directions for the psychoanalytic psychology of religion, initiating a feminist "analysis" of Freud's cultural texts on religion. By pursuing Freud's analysis of religion, we encounter not only God, but also the absence of God; not only the afterlife, but also the rejection of the afterlife; not only Judaism, but also the loss of Judaism. The absence of religion thus proves as significant as its presence in Freud's work.

This introduction situates the project in relation to other feminist responses to Freud in religious studies. In addition, it describes the tenacity of the Oedipal masterplot in Freud's work and suggests how his incompletely developed counterthesis enables a feminist analysis and critique of misogyny and xenophobia in culture and the unconscious. The first chapter exposes the counterthesis in both an early text, *The Interpretation of Dreams,* and the much later "A Religious Experience." At sites that bracket the entire span of Freud's career, the limitations, interruptions, and subversions of the Oedipal masterplot, the points at which Freud turned aside from Oedipal interpretation, thus become evident.

The second chapter focuses specifically on the themes of death, immortality, and the afterlife, revealing in Freud's texts, in addition to an Oedipal theory of patricidal fantasies, a set of images involving dead mothers, mothers as instructors in death, and "uncanny" (*unheimlich*) maternal bodies. Freud's analysis of "the uncanny" as a term which "comes to mean its opposite" is pivotal for the counterthesis. Death, immortality, and the mother's body are all described as "(un)canny": Freud used similar terminology to describe the fantasy of a heavenly afterlife, a "home in the uncanny," and the genitals of the mother, an "uncanny home."

The third chapter turns to the notion of the "uncanny Jew" as a widespread trope in Central Europe and as a subtext in Freud's essay "The Uncanny." Freud initiated a fragmentary analysis of the unconscious intersections of Jewishness, assimilation, death, and the mother in which the (un)canniness or *(Un)Heimlichkeit* of Jewishness to Jews is a central theme. This becomes evident in Freud's writings on his own Jewish identity, especially through an analysis of two presentations to a Viennese Jewish men's group, the B'nai B'rith, to which Freud belonged for many years.

The fourth chapter examines Freud's comments on the entanglement of anti-Semitism with misogyny. Freud's description of castration anxiety and circumcision as central to both the fear of the Jew and the fear of the mother leads to a set of speculations on the "abject" as the source of both xenophobia and misogyny.

The fifth chapter turns to two texts written in 1915, reflections on mourning and melancholia, showing that the themes of the uncanny mother and Jewish identity lie just below the surface of these texts. Freud here shows himself as a successful mourner of religion in transition, but an unsuccessful or "melancholic" mourner of the lost mother. Freud's inability to mourn the mother is far from idiosyncratic, however, for we are all melancholy mourners of maternal loss. Freud's incomplete forays into this terrain offer fragmentary and provocative interpretations of the unconscious associations of mortality and maternity and a promising step toward bringing to consciousness the sources of the twin plagues of misogyny and xenophobia.

The epilogue moves beyond Freud, raising questions about the forms taken by the counterthesis in contemporary culture and asking how our expressions of the counterthesis can be transformed from rage and hostility into awareness and reconciliation. Anti-abortion web sites on the Internet today provide a vivid illustration of the counterthesis in contemporary culture: dangerous and deadly mothers, in the rhetoric of the web sites, are closely associated with immortality, and Holocaust imagery appears in projected and distorted form. Yet acknowledgment of the "unspeakable" of the counterthesis may offer the possibility of reconciliation between the opposing voices in the abortion debates. Concluding remarks consider the implications of Freud's counterthesis for the study of religion in modernity.

FEMINISM, FREUD, AND THE STUDY OF RELIGION

Freud has been criticized frequently, and correctly, for the male bias or androcentrism of his Oedipal theory of religion and culture. Without doubt, his Oedipal paradigm situates woman in a secondary role. She is the object of incestuous desire in the fantasy of the male child, she is a morally inferior being without a strong superego, and she is excluded from the work of culture. The Oedipal theory, many have argued, rests upon an assumption of female inferiority. Freud's analyses, these theorists conclude, seem to support a broad-based misogynist ideology. His remarks on the origins of religion and morality in *The Ego and the Id* are often cited as illustrations of this Oedipal androcentrism: "Religion, morality, and a social sense — the chief elements in the higher side of man — were ... acquired phylogenetically out of the father-complex ... the male sex seems to have taken the lead in all these moral acquisitions" (*SE* 19: 37; see Rizzuto 1979: 42). Similarly, many have pointed critically to Freud's remarks in *Civilization and Its Discontents* suggesting that women are the enemies of culture. Less capable than men of renunciation and sublimation, Freud argued, women "come into opposition to civilization and display their retarding and restraining influence." Instead, "the work of civilization has become increasingly the business of men, it confronts them with ever more difficult tasks and compels them to carry out instinctual sublimations of which women are little capable" (*SE* 21: 103). This exclusion of women from the "capacity for cultural production" has troubled feminists for generations (Garner 1985: 29). From this critical feminist perspective, Freud is seen as a misogynist thinker.

Nor have Freud's speculations about morality and gender escaped critique. Many have noted the androcentrism in his assessment of women's morality in "Some Psychical Consequences of the Anatomical Distinction between the Sexes," where he states, "I cannot evade the notion (though I hesitate to give it expression) that for women the level of what is ethically normal is different from what it is in men. Their super-ego is never so inexorable, so impersonal, so independent of its emotional origins as we require it to be in men" (*SE* 19: 257; see Van Herik 1982).

In Freud's Oedipal writings on civilization, religion, and morality, then, his androcentrism stands out in vivid relief. The psychologist of religion David Wulff summarizes the foundations of the feminist critique: "Freud's psychology of religion is . . . clearly centered in masculine reactivity. It is the male's ambivalent relationship with his father, both in his own and in the race's childhood, that lies at the core of religion as Freud views it" (Wulff 1997: 285). This androcentrism is clearly evident in Freud's Oedipal analyses of religion. His critics are correct to challenge and critique his approach. Freud's texts, however, can be read in other ways. My project is what I call "analytic," rather than "critical" or "inclusive" (Jonte-Pace 1997b, 2001).

Feminist scholars have reacted to Freud's androcentric accounts of culture and religion in one of these three major ways. Feminist "critical" reactions have challenged psychoanalysis for its androcentrism, dismissing Freud for constructing a virtually "womanless" theory, for assuming masculine normativity, and for portraying women as physically, morally, and intellectually deficient (Friedan 1963, Millet 1970, Greer 1971, Sprengnether 1990, Kofman 1985, 1991). Sarah Kofman, for example, a French theorist interested in literature, gender, and psychoanalysis, rejects many of Freud's interpretations of literary texts: "If literature, after a reductive treatment, can seem to bend itself to a [psycho]analytic reading, is it not because Freud's conceptions about women coincide with those of the literature that he exploits? An adequation between the literary and the analytic which, far from being an index of truth, is merely an index that both are in the grip of the same cultural and ideological tradition" (1991: 82). According to Kofman and other feminist critics of psychoanalysis, Freud simply perpetuates misogynist cultural ideologies.

Feminist "inclusive" reactions to Freud, on the other hand, seek a psychological theory of religion which incorporates and attends to women's knowledge and experience. These theorists have often turned away from Freud and toward the alternative methodologies developed by object-relations theorists (Winnicott 1972, Klein 1975) and self psychologists (Kohut 1971). This vein of psychoanalytic feminism attends to the maternal-infant bond in the earliest, "pre-Oedipal" months of life (Chodorow 1978, 1989, Benjamin 1988, Flax 1990, Sprengnether 1990).[2] Mary Ellen Ross and Cheryl Lynn Ross, for example, argue that many aspects of religious ritual and liturgy "can be comprehended within the psychoanalytic interpretation of ritual if such interpretation is extended to include the pre-oedipal period of life" (1983: 27). These authors show that the characteristics of the Roman Catholic Mass "flow from what is essentially an experience of God as Mother" (1983: 39). By investigating the mother-child relationship in the pre-Oedipal period as the psychological source of religious ideas and experiences, feminists have succeeded in avoiding psychoanalytic androcentrism by developing more "inclusive" psychologies of religion, ritual, morality, and belief (Gilligan 1984, Ross and Ross 1983, Jonte-Pace 1987, 1993, Jones 1996, Lutzky 1991, Raab 1997, Goldenberg 1990).

Feminist theorists in the psychology of religion who pursue the "analytic" project, the project which most directly informs this study, have initiated a rather different enterprise. Developing a partnership between psychoanalysis and feminism, these theorists have inquired into the role played by gender in shaping experience and epistemology. They have investigated the cultural construction of gender, and, as theologian Rebecca Chopp puts it, they have examined the ways in which "different categories and structures are marked and constituted through a patriarchal ordering of gender division" (1993: 38). Mari Jo Buhle's volume *Feminism and its Discontents: A Century of Struggle with Psychoanalysis* reflects this analytic perspective, showing that feminism and psychoanalysis have been engaged in a "continuous conversation" about the possibilities for "human liberation" in America throughout the twentieth century (1998: 3).

An important voice in the analytic project is that of Juliet Mitchell. In her groundbreaking *Psychoanalysis and Feminism* (1974), Mitchell cautioned feminist critics against dismissing psychoanalysis, arguing that "psychoanalysis is not a recommendation for a patriarchal society, but an analysis of one." She insisted that "a rejection of psychoanalysis and of Freud's works is fatal for feminism" (1974: xiii). In her view, Freud's goal was to show how a patriarchal culture creates hierarchically gendered beings and how a phallocentric and patricentric world turns infants into gendered women and men. Mitchell suggested that Freud's notion of penis envy, often rejected by feminist critics of psychoanalysis, could be reconceptualized in social and cultural terms. If the phallus is a symbol of the systems of social power and authority from which women in patriarchies are excluded, then penis envy is a way of describing a feminist concern for equality in the social, political, and economic arenas.

Mitchell's concern was to defend Freud's theory of the construction of gender in patriarchal culture. Her focus was not religion. Her work nevertheless points toward new possibilities for the psychology of religion. Influenced by Mitchell's approach, feminist theorists in religious studies have begun to consider how psychoanalysis might provide the methodology appropriate for an analysis of gender, of androcentrism, or of misogyny in religion and culture (Goldenberg 1997).

Julia Kristeva, another analytic theorist well known for her work in feminism and post-structuralism, has introduced into psychoanalytic thinking a concern with the effects of language and power on subjectivity and culture. Many of Kristeva's writings from the 1980s enact feminist revisions of Freud's religious and cultural texts. In *Powers of Horror* (1982), for example, she undertakes a rewriting of Freud's study of the origins of ritual and a rethinking of his interpretation of the sources of anti-Semitism (Jonte-Pace 1997a, 1999b). She goes beyond Freud by pursuing an analysis of the horror of the "maternal abject" at the foundations of the experience of the sacred.

Particularly significant in the "analytic" project is the work of the psychologist of religion Judith Van Herik. In *Freud on Femininity and Faith* (1982), Van Herik examined the role of asymmetrical gender categories in psychoanalysis, demonstrating that in Freud's Oedipal theory of religion, belief is equivalent to femininity, wish fulfillment, and Christianity. Morality, on the other hand, is equivalent to masculinity, the renunciation of wishes, and Judaism. Her work represents a "gender analysis" of belief and morality in Freud's work.

A group of scholars in Jewish cultural studies, among whom are Jay Geller, Sander Gilman, and Daniel Boyarin, has recently produced another set of important feminist analyses of Freud, gender, and religion. The work of these scholars has been instrumental in demonstrating that Freud's writings represent a response to an anti-Semitic ideology widespread throughout fin de siècle Europe within which male Jews were coded as feminine, effeminate, or homosexual. Freud attempted to portray a masculinized Judaism, they suggest, in reaction against this feminization of male Jewishness.

This book is a contribution to the analytic scholarship in the feminist study of religion and psychoanalysis in that it does not simply dismiss Freud as a theorist whose attempt to rethink culture and the unconscious has no relevance for feminism, as the feminist critics of psychoanalysis have done. Nor does it dismiss Freud by looking elsewhere for theoretical models more "friendly" to women, as the inclusivists have done. Instead, it interrogates the Freudian corpus, discovering ways in which it challenges its own hegemony and the hegemony of its culture and uncovering patterns of subversion whereby Freud's counterthesis undermines his own dominant paradigm. This project thus builds upon (and sometimes critiques) the work of Mitchell, Kristeva, Van Herik, Geller, Gilman, and other analytic theorists.

Like Mitchell, I believe that feminists cannot afford to neglect Freud's work. We can benefit from close attention not only to the Oedipal interpretation of the construction of gender in patriarchal culture defended by Mitchell, but also to the associations Freud traced in an incompletely developed non-Oedipal counterthesis. Just as Mitchell reframed the notion of penis envy as a feminist and social category, I suggest a rethinking of the notion of castration anxiety, arguing that it often slips beyond the boundaries of the Oedipal theory into the realm of a pre-Oedipal pattern of misogyny and death anxiety. Like Kristeva, I pursue Freud's deeper insights regarding gender and religion, especially when that pursuit takes us beyond Freud's Oedipal formulations and into the territory of the "abjection" of the maternal which Kristeva finds at the heart of subjectivity, religion, and the sacred. Like Van Herik, I am interested in constructing a feminist analysis of Freud's understanding of gender, religion, and culture. Just as Van Herik's examination of Freud's writings exposed the play of gender in conceptions of belief and morality, my inquiry into Freud's writing exposes the play of gender in fears and fantasies about mortality and immortality, Jewishness and anti-Semitism, secularism and the absence of God. And like Boyarin, Gilman, and Geller, I believe that Freud's writings on culture are best understood by attending to his cultural context. I explore ways in which, as an assimilated (or assimilating) Jew in an anti-Semitic culture, Freud attempted to theorize the gendered dimensions of his own Jewishness and the anti-Semitism of many of his contemporaries: in addition to a "masculinization" of Judaism, Freud's writings also contain an analysis of the associations of the Jew with the feminine or maternal and with death and the uncanny, both for the Jew and for the anti-Semite.

Although Freud is famous for asking the question, "Was will das

Weib?" (What does a woman want?) (Jones 1955: 468), a better formulation of his question is: "What do men *think* that women want?" This
question sometimes takes a related form: "What do men think that
mothers want?" A careful analyst of male fantasies and fears about the
desires of women and mothers, Freud was not unsuccessful at answering these questions. Although he insistently stated that men harbor fantasies of death toward their fathers and sexual desires toward their
mothers, he also, almost unwillingly, inadvertently, or unconsciously,
explored ways in which men wish their mothers dead and fear that
their mothers harbor deadly desires. Freud's theories thus "tell a story
about men's fear of women and the social consequences of that fear"
(Todd 1986: 528).[3]

If Freud's speculations on misogyny can be understood as accurate
accounts of the fantasies of men, are women exempt from these fears
and ideas? I think not. Women within patriarchal societies share, to
some degree, unconscious matriphobic ideas, fantasies, and ideologies
lying below the surface of dominant patriarchal discourses. Freud's
question, as I have revised it, "What do men think that women want?"
can be expanded into the more comprehensive, if less elegant question:
"What do *we men and women fear* that women (and mothers) want?"

Freud's answer to this question is complex. In Freud's texts, male
(and female) fears involving misogyny and matriphobia lie in close
proximity to religious fantasies of immortality and the afterlife, anti-
Semitic and homophobic ideas about degenerate Jews, and fears of
encroaching secularism. These are disturbing notions and fantasies, but
they must be confronted and interrogated. Unconscious misogyny and
xenophobia and their disastrous social consequences will not be eliminated without a careful analysis of their sources and manifestations. As
Harold Bloom has said, "Freud's peculiar strength was to say what
could not be said, or at least to attempt to say it, thus refusing to be silent
in the face of the unsayable" (Bloom 1995: 113). Freud indeed attempted
not only to say the unsayable, but to speak the unspeakable, to say not
merely what cannot be said, but what *must* not be said because it is too

disquieting to confront. In what follows, we read Freud carefully enough to hear not only what he said, but also what he attempted to say.

The unsayable and the unspeakable are dangerous and destructive only as long as they remain unthought, unsaid, or unconscious. Neither unconscious misogyny nor other forms of xenophobia, with all their tragic manifestations, will be eliminated without a careful interrogation of their sources and variations. Nor will conflicts over religion or its absence be resolved by turning away from an awareness of the tenacity of the fantasies and fears underlying religious belief and disbelief. As disturbing as they are, we need not turn away from these images, fantasies, and fears. Speaking the unspeakable about the self in the context of the "talking cure" can produce a liberating or therapeutic awareness of thoughts and memories that would otherwise become pathogenic. Similarly, speaking the unspeakable about culture, religion, and gender can be liberating or healing in broader contexts.

THE UNCONSCIOUS IN BODY, PSYCHE, AND CULTURE

Like Peter Homans (1970, 1989, 1995 [1979]), who reads psychoanalysis as fundamentally a theory about "images, symbol, and myth, about interpretations that presuppose levels of meaning, and about culture" (1970: 14), I read Freud as an interpreter of culture whose insights make sense of symbolic and cultural tensions. Although Freud is sometimes seen as a mechanistic reductionist or as scientist manqué (Jones 1996, Sulloway 1979), he is best read as an analyst of culture, ideology, and the unconscious. He was, of course, trained in the medical and biological science of the late nineteenth century, and the effects of that scientific training are evident throughout his work. But the most important and provocative dimensions of his writings are his formulations of the spaces where the body comes into contact with culture and psyche, where the fears and desires of the unconscious, the demands of civilization, and the "pulsions" of the body intersect (Kristeva 1987).

Freud subjected cultural discourse — religion, folklore, literature — to psychoanalytic interpretation, suggesting that, in the words of Robert Paul, "the symbolism of the unconscious encountered in dreams and neurotic symptoms [is] embedded in the language permeating public cultural discourse" (1991: 267). In addition, he maintained an interest in the way culture provides the system of meanings within which individual development occurs. Although he was deeply concerned with understanding and challenging the effects of cultural constraints on individual behavior, a concern that Foucault dismissed as the "repressive hypothesis" (1980 [1978]: 10–49),[4] he was also attentive to the subtle intersections of cultural, ideological, and unconscious fantasies and desires.[5]

Freud referred often to his project as an investigation of the unconscious in the *Seelenleben* (*SE* 14: 168). Although Strachey translates the term as "mental life" (*SE* 14: 168), a better translation for *Seelenleben* is "psychic life" or "the life of the soul." Freud portrays a "psychic life" in which psyche, body, and culture are closely intertwined. He describes how ideas are shaped, created, and maintained in the unconscious prior to or alongside their enactment in the social arena. Ideas about divine justice, ideas about destiny, death, and the afterlife, ideas about Jewishness, ideas about the presence and absence of God, in Freud's writings, are complex cultural and ideological constructions that resonate with the unconscious fears and desires of individuals. Freud's theory of religion is a theory of how religious ideas are created, experienced, and gendered in the unconscious mind, the *Seelenleben,* and in culture.

I read Freud, then, as an interpreter of personal and cultural fantasies, a reader of psychic realities, an excavator of the unconscious. The fantasies of individuals and the ideologies of cultures, viewed through a psychoanalytic lens, can be seen as obscure revelations of unconscious psychological activities. Reading Freud as a theorist of culture and of the unconscious, I approach his writings on religion as attempts to formulate the workings of the unconscious in religious and cultural ideas and to expose the psychic realities underlying religious concepts. While Freud's work is not beyond critique, his theories of culture have only begun to be tapped. His counterthesis has lain undeveloped beneath the Oedipal masterplot, its rich implications, both for challenging his dominant arguments and for interpreting culture, unexamined.

Feminists must use caution against facile engagements with master discourses, for indeed, as Tina Chanter asks, "How are we to weigh the strategic gains to be had from positioning oneself in relation to a master discourse, even if one looks on it askance? Are the losses we incur too great, or is this a risk worth taking?" (Chanter 1995: 216).[6] Such a risk is, in fact, worth taking in relation to Freud's "master discourse." In this book, I set out to demonstrate powerful contradictions, gaps, and inconsistencies deeply embedded in Freud's theories. My goal in focusing on them is not to join in the condemnation of Freud's theories so common in the contemporary era, but rather to argue that these contradictions are meaningful. As Freud himself said in another context, "these contradictions stand in need of an explanation" (*SE* 5: 514).

THE TENACITY OF THE OEDIPAL MASTERPLOT

The centrality of the Oedipus complex in psychoanalytic theory is indisputable. It provides not only a paradigm for the structure of the psyche, but also a system for the evaluation of culture. Freud himself called the Oedipus complex "the shibboleth that distinguishes the adherents of psychoanalysis from its opponents" (*SE* 7: 226 n. 1). It has been called Freud's "greatest discovery" (Rudnytsky 1987: x) and "most important paradigm" (Pollock and Ross 1988: xix). It lies "at the heart of Freud's dynamic developmental theory" (Simon and Blass 1991: 161). Freud applied the theory to child development, personality structure, and psychopathology, as well as to the broader phenomena of religious, cultural, and social institutions. In spite of his sometimes dramatic modifications of the Oedipal theory, Freud insisted throughout his life on the accuracy of the Oedipal solution to the riddles he encountered.

Why did Freud turn aside from attempts to speak the unspeakable and fail to confront and develop the non-Oedipal counterthesis that haunts his writings? The answer to this question is complex and overdetermined, but it is possible to isolate some of the intellectual, psychological, and sociohistorical factors. Intellectually, Freud's deep commitment to "uncritical self-observation" came into frequent conflict with his fiercely held sense of the validity of the Oedipal theory (*SE* 4: 103). Psychoanalysis, for Freud, was at the same time method, content, and theory. As an interpretive method, it provides a key to portals otherwise closed to consciousness: it is, as Freud put it, "a procedure for the investigation of mental processes which are almost inaccessible any other way." Second, this method leads to particular contents: it is a description of the contents of the unconscious, a frank and uncensored reportage, a "collection of psychological information" (*SE* 18: 235). Third, it is a theory of the structure or framework — usually Oedipal — within which this collection of psychological information is located and organized.

Freud used psychoanalytic introspection as method fairly carefully, faithfully reporting the results of his excavations of the unconscious in his thinking and writing. While most of the unconscious contents he encountered fell into place as pieces of a coherent theory, some of the pieces simply did not fit the Oedipal puzzle. His attempts to locate these contents within the Oedipal framework were often unsuccessful. His writings are rife with representations that he did not develop into theories, fragments that he was unable to incorporate into his master thesis. In the words of psychoanalyst Didier Anzieu, Freud's work contains images "half glimpsed in the form of thing presentations . . . which he failed to turn into word presentations" (1986: 371).[7]

This tension in the character of psychoanalysis is the context for the counterthesis. Evidence for the counterthesis exists in half-glimpsed images and half-formulated ideas he recorded in numerous texts and documents. Although Freud never fully developed the counterthesis, its traces remain clearly evident in his work in a complex overlapping of one conceptual grid upon another, like the palimpsestic relations of perception and memory that Freud described in his famous essay "A Note upon the Mystic Writing Pad" (*SE* 19: 227). Separating the layers of the "palimpsest" exposes masterplot and counterthesis in tension.[8] The unlayering of this counterthesis relies, in part, on reading Freud in the original German. Many of the connections I make are not apparent in the English translation in the *Standard Edition,* but stand forth vividly in the original language.

The tenacity of the Oedipal masterplot in Freud's theory itself deserves comment. Numerous theories have been proposed to explain Freud's insistence upon Oedipal solutions to life's riddles. Some have focused on Freud's own personal relationships with his mother and father (Sprengnether, Rizzuto, Robert), others on the social and cultural contexts of European anti-Semitism (Gilman, Geller, Boyarin).[9] It is clear that Freud's insistence upon the validity of the Oedipal theory was heavily overdetermined.

One aspect of that overdetermination is that Freud's revelatory sense of the significance of the Oedipal pattern cannot be separated from a personal sense of identification with the Sophoclean Oedipus Rex. Freud's biographer, the psychoanalyst Ernest Jones, recounts a story, now almost legendary, of Freud's sense of identity with Oedipus. In 1906, on his fiftieth birthday, Freud's followers presented him with a medallion engraved on one side with his own portrait and on the other with a design of Oedipus answering the riddle of the Sphinx. Inscribed on the medallion were these words, in Greek, from Sophocles' drama *Oedipus Rex:* "Who knew the famous riddles and was a man most mighty." According to Jones, when Freud read the inscription, he "became pale and agitated . . . as if he had encountered a revenant." The reason for Freud's discomfort, Jones later learned, was that "as a young student at the University of Vienna he used to stroll around the great Court inspecting the busts of former famous professors of the institution. He then had the phantasy . . . of seeing his own bust . . . inscribed with the *identical words* he now saw on the medallion" (Jones

1955: 15; cf. Rudnytsky 1987: 4–5). Freud's fantasized identification with Oedipus was uncannily realized in the gift from his followers.

Freud and Oedipus were both solvers of riddles. The Sphinx had asked Oedipus a riddle requiring an understanding of human change and development: What walks on four, then two, then three legs? Oedipus had answered the Sphinx's riddle, but Freud pursued the riddle further, explaining the gaps in the solution to the riddle, uncovering the hidden history of the creature who walks on four, two, and then three legs. The riddle, in Freud's extension, asked how the transitions occur. What enables the creature to move from infancy to adulthood? What causes the creature to limp in old age? Freud's answer to the riddle Oedipus had only begun to answer was, of course, Oedipus himself: the Oedipus complex, the love of the mother and the hatred of the father, moves the creature from infancy to adulthood. The Oedipus complex wounds and limits the creature. The Oedipus complex leads inevitably to the sufferings and infirmities of old age. Oedipus had begun to answer the Sphinx's riddle, but Freud felt that he himself had completed the puzzle, solving the riddle once and for all. Freud, like Oedipus, "knew the famous riddles and was a man most mighty."

Freud encountered many riddles during his career. He argued that most riddles are Oedipal riddles: he suggested, for example, that the first problem encountered by children, "the riddle of where babies come from," is, in a distorted form, "the same riddle that was propounded by the Theban Sphinx" (*SE* 7: 195). He enjoyed using the rhetoric of the riddle *(das Rätsel)* in his writing. He struggled with "the riddle of the nature of femininity" (*SE* 22: 113), and he expressed bewilderment in the face of the riddle of mourning, proclaiming "to psychologists, mourning is a great riddle" (*SE* 14: 306). In autobiographical remarks incorporated into a postscript to "The Question of Lay Analysis," he described his lifelong desire to "understand something of the riddles of the world in which we live and perhaps even to contribute something to their solution" (*SE* 20: 253). Similarly, he posed questions about the riddle of faith and belief: "as though the world had not riddles enough, we are set the new problem of understanding how these other people have been able to acquire their belief in the Divine Being" (*SE* 23: 123).

Although he wished to believe that most riddles are variants of the riddle posed to Oedipus by the Sphinx and that their solutions are Oedipal, as well, even Freud knew that some riddles escape Oedipal solutions. So deeply attached was Freud, both intellectually and psychologically — and politically, as Schorske (1973), McGrath (1986), and others have shown — to the notion that the Oedipal complex must be correct, however, that he was only occasionally able to perceive the rich counterthesis within his own sights. His images and metaphors reveal the tenacity with which he held to the Oedipal theory, the way it functioned as an "unshakable bulwark" against alternate views (Freud, in Jung 1963: 149).

Yet this bulwark was not truly unshakable. Noting occasionally the limitations of the Oedipal paradigm, Freud initiated a trajectory contradictory to his Oedipal analyses of the origins of religion, morality, and monotheism in primal parricides. Characterized by fears and fantasies focused on a dead or deadly mother, the counterthesis constructs a fragmentary theory of death, immortality, and the afterlife, a tentative analysis of the canniness of Jewish identity to the Jew and the uncanniness of the Jew to the anti-Semite, and a hesitant analysis of the loss of religion and the absence of God.

CHAPTER I

The Counterthesis in "The Dream Book" and "A Religious Experience"

The Beginning and End of Interpretation

On November 19, 1899, about two weeks after the publication of *The Interpretation of Dreams,* Freud wrote impatiently to his friend Wilhelm Fliess in Berlin, "It is a thankless task to enlighten mankind a little. No one has yet told me that he feels indebted to me for having learned something new from the dream book and for having been introduced to a world of new problems" (Masson 1985: 387). Although it took longer than two weeks for the world to realize that Freud had "enlightened mankind a little" with what he called his "dream book," we now understand that he did indeed introduce to our century a "world of new problems."

Some parts of this world of new problems, however, have barely been visited in a century of readings. Freud's justly famous book *The Interpretation of Dreams* and his less well-known essay "A Religious Experience" provide "specimen texts" for an inquiry that does so, somewhat like the "specimen dream" Freud described and interpreted in the second chapter of his dream book. This chapter begins by describing and interpreting two key moments in *The Interpretation of Dreams,* suggesting that the more visible framework for the volume is undercut by an interruptive counterthesis which subverts the masterplot by acknowledging its limitations, both implicitly and explicitly. Freud's text not only provides a cartography for the "royal road to the unconscious," but simultaneously deconstructs its own cartography at sites Freud described as the beginning and the end of interpretation. This beginning and end coincide with the encounter with religion and the maternal body. A discussion of a dream from the dream book and a crisis of faith from "A Religious Experience" will conclude the chapter, showing how the presence of the dead mother, like the points marking the beginning and end of interpretation, subverts the Oedipal masterplot.

ON THE ROYAL ROAD: "ACHERONTA MOVEBO"

Devoting an entire chapter of his mid-twentieth-century biography of Freud to *The Interpretation of Dreams,* Ernest Jones applauds the volume as Freud's most important, best-known, and most original work, the work which would bring him lasting fame. "By general consensus," he says, "*The Interpretation of Dreams* was Freud's major work, the one by which his name will probably be longest remembered" (1953: 384). Emphasizing the Oedipal themes in the work, Jones states, "the description of the now familiar 'Oedipus complex,' the erotic and the hostile relations of child to parent, are frankly exposed" (384).

Jones is correct, of course, to emphasize the significance of the work. The impact of Freud's dream book on our century is indisputable. At the opening of the twenty-first century, we all "speak Freud," as Peter Gay has said (1999: 69), and in large part, the dream book is responsible for this new language. Jones is correct, as well, to point out Oedipal themes in the volume. Although Oedipus became associated with a "complex" in Freud's work only in 1910, *The Interpretation of Dreams* was the text in which Freud first published the Oedipal theory. And although Oedipus did not make an appearance until nearly halfway through the volume (*SE* 5: 261), Freud commented on "Oedipus dreams" in a section on "typical dreams" (*SE* 5: 398). He also devoted several pages to an interpretation of Sophocles' play *Oedipus Rex,* and he quoted Sophocles' famous words, "many a man 'ere now in dreams hath lain with her who bare him" (*SE* 4: 264). Letters to Wilhelm Fliess during the years he was writing the book document his sense of the centrality of Oedipus in its argument. He first outlined the "dream book" to Fliess in a letter of March 1898, describing his intention to incorporate in the six chapters "comments on *Oedipus Rex,* the talisman fairy tale, and possibly *Hamlet.*" He added, "I first must read up on the Oedipus legend — do not yet know where" (Masson 1985: 304).

Yet Freud introduced the book not with a motto from Sophocles' famous account of the tragic Oedipal legend, but rather with a reference to another legendary tale from the ancient world, Virgil's heroic saga of the founding of the city of Rome. On the frontispiece of *The Interpretation of Dreams* and again in the final pages of the book, Freud quoted Virgil's words from the *Aeneid:* "Flectere si nequeo superos, Acheronta movebo" (If I cannot bend the Higher Powers, I will move the Infernal Regions) (*SE* 5: 608).[1] Freud understood the passage as a reference to the path of repressed instinctual impulses (*SE* 5: 608 n. 1), and thus, as a reference to repressed fantasies, Oedipal and otherwise, in the unconscious. It is also a self-reflexive comment. By selecting this epigraph, Freud suggested that he, in his quest for the meanings of dreams, would stir up the deepest layers, the lowest regions of the underworld or unconscious. His Oedipal masterplot is, in a sense, contained within Virgil's famous evocation of the journey to the depths.[2] So, however, is the counterthesis we shall explore: what Freud stirred up in the Infernal Regions of the unconscious was more than just Oedipal.

In the often-quoted sentence immediately following the Virgilian passage, Freud continued, "The interpretation of dreams is the royal road to a knowledge of the unconscious activities of the mind" (*SE* 5: 608). Freud thus invited the reader to join him on that road. The royal roads of ancient times, however, were direct routes. They were chosen to avoid dangers and obstacles and to maximize administrative efficiency, as Freud, with his interest in the ancient world, no doubt knew. Freud's own sense of the journey to the "infernal regions," however, could not be fully expressed through the metaphor of the "royal road." He thus introduced a competing metaphor of an arduous journey. After a first chapter surveying the literature on dreams and a second offering his "specimen dream," he began the third chapter with these poetic words: "When, after passing through a narrow defile, we suddenly emerge upon a piece of high ground, where the path divides and the finest prospects open up on every side, we may pause for a moment and consider in which direction we shall first turn our steps" (*SE* 4: 122). The narrow defile, the path, and the steps are the classic elements of the ancient pilgrimage or perilous journey. The perilous journey stands in tension with the royal road.

Freud had written to Fliess just a few months before the publication of the dream book describing his intent to structure the volume as a fantasized journey through the wilderness. In a letter of August 6, 1899, he noted, "The whole thing is planned on the model of an imaginary walk. First comes the dark wood of the authorities (who cannot see the trees), where there is no clear view and it is easy to go astray" (*SE* 4: 122 n. 1). Other letters, such as one from July 22, 1899, anticipate the imagery of the "dark forests" of the first chapter: "most readers will get stuck in this thorny thicket *[Dornengestrüpp]*" (Masson 1985: 362–63).[3]

Wittgenstein has called psychoanalysis a "powerful mythology" (1966); Harold Bloom has referred to Freud as "the dominant mythologist of our time" (1995: 113). References to Freud's myth making, if not attempting to discredit psychoanalysis, usually refer to the theory of instincts, which Freud himself called "our mythology" (*SE* 22: 95). Yet Freud is a mythologist in another sense, as well. He draws upon the classic narratives and myths of Western culture to weave his own arguments.

By referring to his text as a dark forest, the middle-aged Freud was drawing a parallel between his book and another epic which begins in a dark wood in midlife. Dante's *Divine Comedy,* like Freud's text, draws heavily upon Virgil's *Aeneid* and starts with the following words: "In the middle of the journey of our life I came to myself within a dark wood *[una selva oscura]* where the straight way was lost" (1:1). Dante's "selva oscura" is the same sort of dark wood in which one loses one's way in Freud's text. Freud was consciously patterning his dream book on Dante's epic as well as on Virgil's.[4] Dante and Virgil describe epic journeys, heroic quests along the path toward truth. But theirs are Roman or Christian journeys, which Freud's is not — and this is a crucial difference. Freud will "take another road" than they followed, "tenere altro viaggio" (1:91), to quote Dante again.[5]

At the beginning of the last chapter of *The Interpretation of Dreams,* Freud reminds his readers of the journey they have accomplished and warns of the ordeals and dangers still to come:

> It will be well to pause and look around, to see whether in the course of our journey up to this point we have overlooked anything of importance. For it must be clearly understood that the easy and agreeable portion of our journey lies behind us. Hitherto . . . all the paths along which we have traveled have led us towards the light — towards elucidation and fuller understanding. But as soon as we endeavor to penetrate more deeply into the mental processes involved in dreaming, every path will end in darkness. (*SE* 5: 511)

These dire warnings of darkness and obscurity at the end of the journey, however, give way to a set of clear instructions on how to overcome the obstacles to understanding the dream, a description of where interpretation begins.

Interpretation begins, he states, at a point of resistance revealed by changes in the dreamer's reiteration of the dream: "If the first account given to me by a patient is too hard to follow, I ask him to repeat it. In doing so he rarely uses the same words. But the parts of the dream which he describes in different terms are by that fact revealed to me as the weak spot in the dream's disguise" (*SE* 5: 515). Describing these

"weak spot[s]" as the point at which interpretation can begin, Freud
uses a significant comparison: these dream sites "serve my purpose just
as Hagen's was served by the embroidered mark on Siegfried's cloak.
That is the point at which the interpretation of the dream can be
started." He continues: "The trouble taken by the dreamer in prevent-
ing the solution of the dream gives me a basis for estimating the care
with which its cloak has been woven" (*SE* 5: 515).

What are the meanings of Siegfried's woven cloak, Hagen's purpose,
and the embroidered mark, in Freud's interpretive project? While the
Virgilian resolve to "move the Infernal Regions" provided the larger
narrative framework for the *Interpretation of Dreams,* Freud introduced
with these references another heroic tale to illustrate the more precise
work of the interpreter: the Germanic *Nibelungenlied,* best known to
Freud and his contemporaries in its Wagnerian form, with its great
adversaries Siegfried and Hagen. Hagen was the legendary slayer of
Siegfried, the hero who could be wounded at only one spot. Hagen is
able to slay the hero because, by trickery, he had persuaded the woman
who "alone knew where the spot was" to indicate the "vital point" with
an embroidered mark (*SE* 5: 515 n. 2). The dream is thus like Siegfried's
woven cloak: the part of the dream where interpretation can begin,
marked by variations in words, is analogous to the embroidered mark
indicating the site of vulnerability. Threads are woven and embroidered into dream cloaks and dream signs. Interpretive swords cut
through woven threads.

Religion is not far from the surface of this text: a heroic Aryan/
Christian/Germanic Siegfried is slain by a stereotypically Jewish antihero, Hagen. Marc Weiner describes Siegfried's Aryan symbolism and
Hagen's Jewishness in Wagner's drama: Siegfried "constitutes a metaphor for the salvation of Germany's future, a salvation based upon racial
exclusion available to the fatherland . . . while Hagen's body is a physi-
ological-metaphorical warning to a Germany that refuses to recognize
the biological dimension of the purported Jewish threat" (1995: 310).[6] In
Freud's comparison, Hagen's purpose, slaying the heroic Siegfried, is

analogous to Freud's purpose, interpreting the dream. Dream interpretation is thus likened to the Jewish antihero's act of killing the hero. It is an act of knowing with religious resonance wherein Jewish interpreters like Freud, with knowledge of secret marks and signs, can perceive hidden desires below "cloaked" surfaces. It implies a position of ultimate power. Through his knowledge of secret marks and signs, the Jewish dream interpreter has power like Hagen's power — the power of death — over others.

In his use of these references, Freud reverses a historical reality: while the mark exposing the Jewishness of the male Jew — the cloaked or clothed mark of circumcision — would give to Germanic anti-Semites the power of life and death over Jews, Freud's hermeneutic exposes what is beneath the woven cloak of the dream, giving power to the Jewish dream interpreter. This also reverses the structure of one of Freud's own well-known narratives involving another Jew on another road also recounted in *The Interpretation of Dreams*. Freud's disillusionment at his father's "unheroic conduct" in the face of the anti-Semitic taunt "Jew, get off the pavement!" (*SE* 4: 197) is countered directly and replaced with its opposite in this narrative of the skilled Jewish interpreter on the royal road who understands the meaning of the embroidered mark on Siegfried's woven cloak. Here, the Jew, master of the royal road, has power, knowledge, and authority: unlike Freud's father, he need not leave the pavement in resignation or defeat. It is no accident that Freud constructed support for his argument through references to Germanic tales in which ambiguous signs expose secret meanings recognizable only to knowledgeable Jewish interpreters. He does not mention explicitly his Jewish identity in these remarks on the "point where interpretation begins," nor does he describe the widespread anti-Semitic assumptions that made Hagen appear Jewish, degenerate, "villainous, and terrifying" (Weiner 1985: 308), but to Freud and his readers, the associations would have been obvious.

Freud's own sense of dream interpretation as a Jewish project is ubiquitous throughout the book and the contemporaneous letters. His frequent references to *The Interpretation of Dreams* as "the Egyptian dream book" or "the Ancient Egyptian Dream Book" in letters to Fliess (Masson 1985: 366, 368) evoke the biblical tale of Joseph, the Jewish interpreter of dreams for the Egyptian pharaoh (Gen. 40–41). On August 6, 1899, for example, he wrote to Fliess "with the most cordial greetings and thanks for your cooperation in the Egyptian dream book" (Masson 1985: 366). Similarly, he asked later that month (August 27): "What would you think of ten days in Rome at Easter (the two of us, of course), if all goes well, if I can afford it and have not been locked up, lynched, or boycotted on account of the Egyptian dream book?" (Masson 1985: 368). A footnote in *The Interpretation of Dreams* corroborates these associations: "It will be noted that the name Josef plays a great part in my dreams. . . . My own ego finds it very easy to hide itself behind people of that name since Joseph was the name of a man famous in the bible as an interpreter of dreams" (*SE* 5: 484 n. 2). His symbolic references to religion thus undergird the text of *The Interpretation of Dreams*.

The heroic nature of the journey into the unconscious and toward the true meaning of dreams is qualified in subtle ways by Freud's allusions. It is a traveling or wandering Jew, not a Virgilian, Oedipal, or Dantean hero, who maps the royal road and reads the hidden signs. Freud's references to himself as Ahasuerus, the eternal wandering Jew, come from later years, but the image lies behind this text, as well. Freud states in a letter to his son Ernst a few days before leaving Vienna for London in May 1938, where he spent his final months: "I sometimes compare myself to old Jacob who, when a very old man, was taken by his children to Egypt. . . . Let us hope that it won't also be followed by an Exodus from Egypt. It is high time that Ahasverus came to rest somewhere" (E. Freud 1992: 298). The heroic adventurer ends his years as a wandering Jew seeking a place of rest.

There is another important dimension to the way Freud narrates the quest for interpretation. In the mythic associations Freud uses to present his theory, Freud's own interpretive identity shifts from the role of hero to the role of antihero or villain. Freud's role is an oppositional one. The Virgilian motto discussed above is actually spoken by Juno, the great goddess who is opposed to Aeneas's heroic quest to establish the city of Rome. In the Virgilian quote, Freud identifies with Juno, the opponent of the heroic adventurer Aeneas, and, in the comparison enlivening the text, with Hagen, the slayer of the heroic Siegfried. Although he had written to Fliess in February 1900, in a letter I discuss further in chapter 3, "I am by temperament nothing but a *conquistador* — an adventurer" (Masson 1985: 398), and although he clearly identified with Oedipus, the heroic solver of riddles, he took, at the same time, an ambivalent stance toward heroic figures, revealing elements of a counterthesis to the masterplot at the very beginnings of interpretation.[7]

If the beginnings of interpretation of the dream are at the site of the saga of the Nibelungen, the ends of interpretation are to be found at the *Nabel,* or navel, of the dream. We noted above that Freud twice quoted Virgil's "Flectere si nequeo superos," once at the beginning and once at the end of the dream book, framing the volume. This doubling is both mirrored and negated in a double reference to the end of interpretation.

The first reference to the end of interpretation appears in a footnote early in the volume: Freud had stated, "There is at least one spot in every dream at which it is unplumbable — a navel as it were *[unergrundlich, gleichsam einen Nabel],* that is its point of contact with the unknown *[mit dem Unerkannten]*" (*SE* 4: 111 n. 1). This "unplumbable" point of contact with the unknown, this dream navel, reappears much later in the volume: there are points, Freud argued, at which the hero must turn aside, the interpreter must look away:

> There is often a passage in even the most thoroughly interpreted dream, which has to be left obscure *[man muss oft eine Stelle im Dunkel lassen];*[8] this is because we become aware during the work of interpretation that at that point there is a tangle *[Knäuel]* of dream-thoughts which cannot be unraveled *[der sich nicht entwirren will]* and which moreover adds nothing to our knowledge of the

content of the dream. This is the dream's navel *[der Nabel des Traums]*, the spot where it reaches down into the unknown *[Unerkannten]*. (*SE* 5: 525)

Freud continues this paragraph with a different metaphor for dream thoughts. Here they are infinitely branching, rather than tangled: "the dream thoughts to which we are led by interpretation cannot, from the nature of things, have any definite endings; they are bound to branch out in every direction into the intricate network *[netzartige Verstrickung]* of our world of thought. It is at some point where this meshwork *[Geflecht]* is particularly close that the dream-wish grows up, like a mushroom out of its mycelium" (*SE* 5: 525). Regardless of the ever-branching pattern of meshworks or networks in the dream thoughts, however, some dreams are impenetrable, some unknowns unknowable, some tangles unravelable.

What leads Freud to turn away at the "navel of the dream"? What is the "unknown" that he finds unfathomable, impenetrable, or "un-plumbable"? His own imagery is evocative. The navel of the dream, the spot where it "reaches . . . into the unknown," evokes the human navel, the bodily mark of the passage through the maternal genitals and into the world. The interpretation of the dream, which began at the point of the embroidered mark where Hagen slew Siegfried, must come to an end at another mark, the birthmark, the scar that marks the site of the connection to and separation from the mother. It is the site of connection to and separation from the mother that Freud cannot interpret. Freud's turning aside at the "navel of the dream" is, in a sense, an acknowledgment of the limitations of the heroic paths of figures like Oedipus and Aeneas. As such, it marks a moment at which Freud encounters and retreats from the limits of the Oedipal masterplot. The point at which interpretation must end is both navel and knot, birthmark and tangle of threads. Both navel *(Nabel)* and tangle *(Knäuel)* interrupt the saga of the Nibelungen, or the journey of the hero.

Freud's references to the intricate "network" or "meshwork" or the "tangle of dream thoughts which cannot be unraveled" are as evocative as his reference to the "dream navel." Like Homer, who interrupts the saga of Ulysses' journey with the narrative of Penelope's woven and unwoven tapestry, Freud recounts a story of an interpretive excursus interrupted by threads, weavings, and tangles. As we have seen, his remarks on the beginnings of interpretation involve woven cloths, dream cloaks, and embroidered marks. His comments on the ends of interpretation involve unwoven tangles of threads and words, points at which dream thoughts become networks or meshworks of threads. The rhetoric of thread, knot, and weaving is dense.[9]

What is this unravelable tangle that brings about the end of interpretation?[10] Following the threads, we note that twenty years after the publication of *The Interpretation of Dreams,* Freud wrote a short essay (published posthumously after yet another twenty years had passed) about another tangle of threads. Here, in "Medusa's Head," a text I discuss further in chapter 2, Freud identifies the tangle. The unravelable tangle in "Medusa's Head" and the tangle in *The Interpretation of Dreams* is the hair which covers the "dangerous" genitals of the mother: "Medusa's head takes the place of a representation of the female genitals ... it isolates their horrifying effects from their pleasure-giving ones" (*SE* 18: 274). This tangle is also one at which the hero must turn away: Perseus, the heroic slayer of the Medusa, cannot look directly at her face, lest he be paralyzed.[11]

Like Perseus, Freud averted his eyes from the psychoanalyst's task of interpretation when the task involved unraveling the threads that led to the mother's body. Freud's words represent an acknowledgment of the limitations of the Oedipal master thesis. He turned away at the tangle of maternal hair and at the navel, the site of the scar memorializing the loss of the mother through the cutting of the cord which once linked infant to mother, for he knew that the Oedipal road, the royal road, although it theorizes an erotic reunion with the mother, could not take him to this uncanny destination. Indeed, this navel, which is a point of contact with the "unknown" *(Unerkannten),* which "has to be left obscure" (*SE* 5: 525) may in fact be the same "Great Unknown" *(Grosse Unerkannten)* Freud identified with Death in a dream interpretation a few pages earlier (*SE* 5: 472).

Freud's footnote on the "unplumbable navel" of the dream is situated within his interpretation of the "specimen dream," the famous dream of Irma's injection which introduces the interpretive method of the "dream book." In Freud's associations to the dream, he found three women: "I had been comparing my patient Irma with two other people. . . . If I had pursued my comparison between the three women, it would have taken me far afield. There is at least one spot in every dream at which it is unplumbable — a navel, as it were, that is its point of contact with the unknown" (*SE* 4: 110, 111 n. 1). The three women he does not pursue are Irma (who was in reality, at the time Freud dreamed this significant dream, near death because of surgical malpractice on the part of Freud's friend, Fliess), a friend of Irma's, and Freud's wife. Freud backed away from an interpretation of these three women, saying that he "had a feeling that the interpretation of this part of the dream was not carried far enough to make it possible to follow the whole of its concealed meaning" (*SE* 4: 111 n. 1). As we will see in chapter 2, Freud ventured, in other texts and other decades, into this dangerous territory of female triads. The three women in "The Theme of the Three Caskets," for example, are closely associated with death, the absence of God, and the fantasy of immortality. In his interpretation of this dream, however, he can only turn aside, looking away from the uncanny navel in a gesture that repeats his acknowledgment of the limitations of the Oedipal perspective.[12]

The navel and the tangle as references to the body of the mother and to death signal the "end of interpretation," the place where the telos, the "end" or goal of interpretation, gives way to its "end" or abandonment. From an Oedipal perspective, Freud should not turn away from the fantasy of the mother's body. But the navel and the tangle do not invite or entice: in Freud's words, they produce "horror," or *Grauen*. They are the unspeakable. Elsewhere, less fettered by attachments to royal roads and heroic journeys, he attempted hesitant unravelings of these tangled threads, exploring tentatively the dream's "point of contact with the unknown." These efforts are not unrelated to his attempts to plumb other "unknowns" and to solve other riddles, such as mortality, immortality, the afterlife, the psyche of the Jew, and the anxiety of the anti-Semite.

In his dream book, then, Freud invites the reader to accompany him on a journey which, at first glance, appears to be both a regal excursion to the unconscious in order to discover Oedipal wishes and desires, or a heroic journey overcoming all obstacles to penetrate the hidden secrets of dreams. But the beginning and end of interpretation point in different directions than the Oedipal journey. At the beginning of interpretation, woven threads mark the site at which Jewish dream interpreters are metaphorically identified with slayers of legendary heroes at points marked by woven and embroidered threads. At the end of interpretation, we encounter insurmountable obstacles where the body of the mother lies hidden behind the navel of the dream and the tangle of dream thoughts. These tangles and obstacles are hints of Freud's awareness of the limitations of the Oedipal paradigm. He encounters and retreats from elements of a subversive counterthesis within the larger narrative framework by drawing connections between the methods of the (Jewish) dream interpreter and the actions of the antihero who slays Siegfried and also by approaching, then turning away from, the body of the mother.

Freud's double articulation in *The Interpretation of Dreams* of the famous Virgilian passage "Flectere si nequeo superos, Acheronta movebo" as an expression of masterplot and royal road is thus countered by his double acknowledgment of the limits of interpretation in the two passages on the "navel of the dream" and by his account of Siegfried's murder as a way to characterize the method of dream interpretation. Although the dream book maps the royal road, the masterplot is subtly subverted, both at the point where interpretation begins and at the "point of contact with the unknown," the navel of the dream where interpretation must end.

TURNING AWAY AT THE BODY OF THE MOTHER

The counterthesis interrupts the Oedipal masterplot at the site of the body of the dead mother. This mother appears in numerous texts and is discussed further in chapter 2, but two brief examples suffice to introduce her here: Freud's short essay "A Religious Experience," written in 1928, shortly after the publication of *The Future of an Illusion,* and a childhood dream of Freud's, recounted in *The Interpretation of Dreams.* At each of these sites, a dead mother is central; immortality, an absent God, and the afterlife are prominent themes; and a cover-up of sorts occurs: the presence of death is denied as the dead mother is replaced by an erotic mother. Just as in the end of interpretation in *The Interpretation of Dreams,* Freud turns away from the maternal body. A seemingly impenetrable Oedipal analysis, upon closer inspection, reveals itself to be full of cracks and contradictions. These expose a counterthesis below the surface of the text.

Troubled by a published interview (Viereck 1930) in which Freud had described his lack of religious faith and his "indifference on the subject of survival after death," an American doctor initiated a correspondence with Freud, sharing with him the story of his religious crisis and conversion. His hope was to induce Freud to "open his mind" to God and to the truths of Christianity. "What struck me most," the doctor said in his letter to Freud, "was your answer to the question whether you believe in a survival of personality after death. You are reported as having said 'I give no thought to the matter'" (*SE* 21: 169).

The catalyst in the doctor's crisis of faith had been the dead body of a woman. In his letter to Freud, he explained the onset of his sudden religious doubts: "one afternoon while I was passing through the dissecting room my attention was attracted to a sweet-faced dear old woman who was being carried to a dissecting table. This sweet-faced woman made such an impression on me that a thought flashed through my mind: 'There is no God'" (*SE* 21: 170).

The American doctor reported not only upon the "dark night of his soul" and his overpowering feeling of the absence of God, but also upon the resolution of his crisis. Some time after the sight of the dead woman and the painful emergence of doubt and disbelief, consolation came to him: "God made it clear to my soul that the Bible was His Word, that the teachings about Jesus Christ were true.... Since then God has revealed Himself to me by many infallible proofs." Echoing and transforming Freud's own phrase, "I give no thought to the matter," the physician begged him to "give thought to this most important matter" and to share in his journey from disbelief to belief (*SE* 21: 169–70).

For Freud, this narrative provided rich material for Oedipal analysis. Where the American doctor saw a dead woman and felt the absence of God, Freud's interpretation transformed the dead woman into an erotic mother and the absent God into a hated father. In Freud's interpretation,

> the sight of a woman's dead body, naked or on the point of being
> stripped, reminded the young man of his mother. It roused in him
> a longing for his mother which sprang from his Oedipus complex,
> and this was immediately completed by a feeling of indignation
> against his father. His ideas of "father" and "God" had not yet
> become widely separated; so that his desire to destroy his father
> could become conscious as doubt in the existence of God and could
> seek to justify itself in the eyes of reason as indignation about the ill
> treatment of a mother object. (171)

While the American doctor's own explanation of his return to religious belief emphasized the role of divine intervention, Freud attempted a classically Oedipal explanation. The abandonment of incestuous wishes for the mother and submission to the authority of the father, Freud argued, is recapitulated in the doctor's abandonment of disbelief: "The outcome of the struggle was displayed once again in the sphere of religion and it was of a kind predetermined by the fate of the Oedipus complex: complete submission to the will of God the father" (171). For Freud, the analysis was simple: incestuous wishes of the American doctor led to fantasies of parricide which took the form of deicide, and fears of divine retribution led to the renunciation of deicidal fantasies.

Freud thus leaves the reader with a parsimonious and apparently seamless analysis of an American doctor's crisis of faith, but some discontinuities remain in the text. Freud fails to incorporate certain seemingly obvious Oedipal elements from the doctor's account, and he dismisses certain elements which would seem to fall outside of Oedipal territory. The obvious Oedipal element in the doctor's account which Freud fails to theorize is the pivotal theme upon which much of psychoanalytic theory turns: the idea of the absence of the phallus, typically described in terms of castration anxiety. As is well known, Freud held that in the male child's Oedipal development, the child is moved to renounce incestuous wishes by castration anxiety. Whether castration anxiety is introduced by an explicit paternal threat or whether it emerges as a result of the shock of seeing the female genitals, the fear of castration motivates renunciatory morality (*SE* 19: 173–79, 248–58). The child renounces his desire to possess the mother and to destroy the father, establishing the possibility of a lifelong pattern of obedience to figures of authority.

The castrative element in this essay is not difficult to discern — the sight of the dead woman on the way to the dissecting table is not only the catalyst for disbelief, she is also the catalyst for the return to belief. She is triply castrated: she is female, she is dead, and she is about to be dissected. The "sweet-faced old woman" is a multivocal embodiment of castration imagery, lacking the penis, lacking life, and under the knife. But this pivotal piece of Oedipal material is excised, as it were, from the analysis. Freud missed a significant opportunity to sharpen an Oedipal argument. The fact that the dead mother in this text lies in close proximity to God and the afterlife — and to the absence of God — complicates her Oedipal credentials.

At the same time, the dead mother pointed Freud toward phenomena that the Oedipal theory could not easily explain, elements of the experience that Freud swept aside with his neat Oedipal explanation. As we shall see, the dead mother can invoke not only Oedipal, castrative anxieties, but also anxieties centering on fragmentation, abandonment, matriphobia, and matricide. Fantasies of dead mothers thus express an ambivalence toward maternal figures which Freud was unable fully to articulate or analyze. But an absent God, a dead mother, and a sense of anxiety over mortality and the afterlife also are elements of the counterthesis I am tracing. In that counterthesis, ambivalence toward the mother — and matricidal fantasies — are more significant and more prominent than the Oedipal dynamics of erotic love toward mothers.

Freud's short essay linking death, mothers, and concern over the afterlife, then, contains a narrative of doubt and resolution (in the American doctor's letter) and a narrative of interpretation and analysis (in the Viennese doctor's text). In both narratives, the death-woman connection is crucial: both doctors encounter death in the guise of a mother, and both displace the dead women. In one narrative, the dead mother is displaced as the doctor follows a religious trajectory from doubt to belief in God and the afterlife. In the other, she is displaced as Freud follows an interpretive trajectory from incestuous, Oedipal desire to its renunciation. The American doctor's narrative of conversion moves from death, absence, woman, and disbelief (or the nonexistence of God) to the antitheses of these: eternal life, divine presence, God the Father, and belief. The doctor's text constructs religion in gendered categories of presence and absence: an absence which is gendered as feminine gives way to a presence which is gendered as masculine (Jonte-Pace 1992: 14–17, 1996).

Freud's parallel narrative in "A Religious Experience," however, transforms the dead woman of the doctor's account not into an absent and then present divine Father, but into a living, desirable mother: maternal absence becomes erotic maternal presence.[13] Each doctor felt he had the last word — the American doctor offered words of prayer, assuring Freud that petitions "were being earnestly addressed to God ... that he might grant [him] faith to believe" (*SE* 21: 170). The Viennese doctor offered words of interpretation. The dead woman,

Freud reiterates in the last lines of the essay, was the key to the analysis. Her absent presence or present absence was the "particular determining event which caused the subject's skepticism to flare up for a last time before being finally extinguished" (*SE* 21: 172). Freud's rhetoric and imagery emphasize the finality of his interpretation and echo the finality of death. God and the fantasy of immortality, Freud maintains, are illusory. Psychoanalysis, on the other hand, is immortal and true.[14]

The interpretive debate between a Christian doctor and an atheist psychoanalyst also brings into focus another factor: Freud's Jewish identity. Freud's Jewishness is very much in evidence in "A Religious Experience." The text is, in a sense, a recapitulation of an old story of tensions between Christians and Jews, modified by Freud's self-identification as a scientist, atheist, and psychoanalyst, as well as a Jew.

On the surface, Freud gives us a simple narrative: an atheist expresses his disbelief, a Christian expresses a wish to convert him, and the atheist rejects the attempt at conversion using the encounter as an opportunity for Oedipal interpretation. What stands out clearly upon closer inspection, however, is that the atheist defends himself against conversion by reference specifically to his Jewish identity. After recounting the American doctor's earnest efforts to induce him to "open his mind" to religious truths, Freud states wryly,

> I sent a polite answer saying that I was glad to hear that this experience had enabled him to retain his faith. As for myself, God had not done so much for me. He had never allowed me to hear an inner voice; and if, in view of my age, he did not make haste, it would not be my fault if I remained to the end of my life what I now was — an "infidel Jew." (*SE* 21: 170)

The Christian doctor responded to Freud by insisting that, in spite of his Jewishness, conversion was still a possibility: "my colleague gave me an assurance that being a Jew was not an obstacle in the pathway to true faith and proved this by several instances" before offering prayers for Freud's conversion (170).

The efforts of the pious American proselyte for Christianity are dismissed with irony before Freud initiates his psychoanalytic interpretation: "I am still awaiting the outcome of this intercession" (170). Freud, of course, is something of a proselyte for psychoanalysis here: he wishes to convince and convert his readers of the rationality of atheism and the accuracy of his psychoanalytic interpretation of the Christian's crisis of faith. But Freud's Jewish identity is neither a peripheral theme in this text nor merely an opportunity for humor at the expense of the American doctor. Freud's resistance to the castrative interpretation noted above is due in part to a sense of the symbolic Jewishness of the figure whose presence led to the crisis of faith. The knife of the dissecting table echoes the knife used in circumcising Jewish boys. The identity of dead mother is uncomfortably close to the identity of the "infidel Jew."

Freud resists this disturbing parallel through his use of gently mocking humor at the expense of the American doctor. It may be relevant to note that, in "Humour," an essay written almost simultaneously with this one,[15] Freud described the Oedipal foundations of the type of humor which makes one person the object of another's amusement or derision. When one "is made the object of humorous contemplation by the other," the narrator behaves "as an adult does towards a child when he recognizes and smiles at the triviality of interests and sufferings which seem so great to it. Thus the humorist would acquire his superiority by . . . identifying himself to some extent with his father" (*SE* 21: 161, 163). Freud's wry and mocking remarks at the expense of the earnest American doctor thus reflect his efforts to maintain the Oedipal framework. At the same time, they recapitulate his Oedipal interpretation of the doctor's crisis of faith.

But the doubling of the Oedipal emphasis through humor and through interpretation itself does not succeed at covering the gaps in the Oedipal argument. What Freud avoided mentioning in this text — castration anxiety — is associated not only with the dead mother discussed above, but also with the circumcision of the Jewish male. Freud's analyses, in other texts, of the uncanniness of circumcision and the unconscious conflation of circumcision and castration (which will be discussed in chapter 4),[16] represent deeper efforts at pursuing these connections. But in this particular essay, "A Religious Experience," Freud, the Jewish atheist, avoids any discussion of what would seem to be a crucial piece of his argument. His resistance here provides a hint of the counterthesis.

In *The Interpretation of Dreams,* we find a childhood dream which resonates powerfully with the imagery and interpretation we have encountered in "A Religious Experience." In this dream, a dead/dying beloved mother with a peaceful, sleeping expression on her features is carried into the room and laid upon a bed. Freud states,

> It is dozens of years since I myself had a true anxiety dream. But I remember one from my 7th or 8th year.[17] . . . I saw my beloved mother, with a peculiarly peaceful, sleeping expression on her features, being carried into the room by two (or three) people with birds' beaks and laid upon the bed. . . . [I thought] my mother was dying. . . . I awoke in anxiety which did not cease till I had woken my parents up. I remember that I suddenly grew calm when I saw my mother's face, as though I had needed to be reassured that she was not dead. (*SE* 5: 583–84)

Freud's account is uncannily similar to his description of the American doctor's experience of the sweet-faced old woman who was carried to the dissecting table.

Freud's interpretation of his own dreamworld encounter is similar to his interpretation of the American doctor's encounter. Seeing a dead mother, they both desired her. His sense of anxiety, he insists, was due to sexual desires, not to wishes or fears of maternal death: "I was not anxious because I had dreamed that my mother was dying. . . . The anxiety can be traced back, when repression is taken into account, to an obscure and evidently sexual craving that had found appropriate expression in the visual content of the dream" (584).[18] Elsewhere in *The Interpretation of Dreams,* Freud had argued that dreaming of the death of "persons of whom the dreamer is fond," especially when feeling "deeply pained by the death," indicates a death wish toward the person: "the meaning of such dreams, as their content indicates, is a wish that the person in question may die" (*SE* 4: 248–49; Atwood and Stolorow 1993: 44). But in the context of this dream, Freud is quick to deny the possibility of matricidal fantasies. The obscure sexual craving for the mother, he insists, is deeper, more primal. The death of the mother is secondary, insignificant, merely an epiphenomenon of preconscious revisions.

But can the dead mother so easily be swept away and replaced by the erotic mother? Can the intimations of a counterthesis be displaced so quickly by the Oedipal master thesis? Psychoanalyst Didier Anzieu is suspicious: "Freud's suggested interpretation of the 'obscure craving' in his dream is unsatisfactory; and the insistence with which he plays down the specific anxiety most prominent in the dream [about the death of his mother] by tracing it back to something else strikes me as suspect" (1986: 308). Psychoanalytic theorist J. B. Pontalis goes further, maintaining that sex is often a kind of cover-up for death in psychoanalytic theory: "The theme of death is as basic to Freudian psychoanalysis as is the theme of sexuality. I even believe that the latter has been widely put forward so as to cover up the former" (1978: 86).

Freud's quick substitution of sex for death stands out as a troubling distortion in both essays. Freud's own remarks about textual distortions may provide a clue to the interpretation of this material. In a discussion of the problem of textual interpretation, he notes, "noticeable gaps, disturbing repetitions and obvious contradictions have come about [in the text], indications which reveal things to us which it was not intended to communicate. In its implications the distortion of a text resembles a murder: the difficulty is not in perpetrating the deed, but in getting rid of its traces" (*SE* 23: 43). In this passage, Freud is alluding to the distortions, repetitions, and contradictions in a paradigmatic text — the Bible — where, as is well known, he did find traces of an unacknowledged murder. Might the same hermeneutic be applied to his own

texts?[19] Might the dead maternal bodies we've found in these texts provide traces which "resemble a murder," a murder that Freud preferred
not to uncover, that is, a fantasy of matricide?

The dead mother and the erotic mother, the mother of the counterthesis and the mother of the masterplot, seem to be inextricably intertwined in "A Religious Experience" and in Freud's childhood dream: "I
thought she was dead and I loved her," Freud seems to say.[20] We find in
each case that he "wanted her dead" in both its matricidal and
necrophiliac senses: he wanted her to die, and he found her erotic and
desirable in death. Feminist theorist Sarah Kofman finds this matricidal
material to be evidence of a deep-seated psychoanalytic misogyny. She
asserts that "psychoanalysis can never touch woman except to make a
dead body of her. To make a dead body of woman is to try one last time
to overcome her enigmatic and ungraspable character. . . . This is a solution to the feminine enigma that is at the very least cheerless, frightening, one that definitively blocks all exits, all paths, all contact" (1985:
223). Post-structuralist psychoanalyst Julia Kristeva, on the other hand,
defends matricidal fantasies as a developmental necessity. "For man and
for woman," Kristeva states, "the loss of the mother is a biological and
psychic necessity, the first step on the way to becoming autonomous.
Matricide is our vital necessity, the sine-qua-non condition of our individuation" (1989: 27–28).

The tension between Kofman's and Kristeva's positions must be
maintained. These fantasies do have harmful social effects upon the
lives of real women, but under our current cultural and developmental
conditions, we cannot do without these fantasies. Both Kofman and
Kristeva are right. Yet both views can be further contextualized: conscious awareness of these unconscious fantasies may enable us to break
their destructive cycles.

Missing from these analyses of fantasies of maternity and mortality,
however, is attention to a third element: immortality. The connection of
death, mothers, and the afterlife is quite evident in "A Religious
Experience." As we noted above, Freud's denial of concern for the

afterlife was the catalyst leading to the American doctor's communications about the dead woman and the absence of God. Freud's childhood dream holds this triad of interrelated ideas, as well. The bird-beaked carriers of the mother, Freud tells us, are associated with images from the illustrated Bible owned by Freud's family. The "strangely draped and unnaturally tall figures with bird's beaks were derived from the illustrations to Philippson's Bible . . . they must have been gods with falcon's heads from an ancient Egyptian funerary relief" (*SE* 5: 583). These funerary illustrations and the biblical text they accompany, the fourth chapter of Deuteronomy (*SE* 5: 583 n. 2), underscore in both image and text the idea of death/immortality and the idea of God's presence/absence. The bird-beaked figures on Egyptian funerary reliefs, as Freud knew, were intended to ensure safe passage of the dead to the afterlife. Freud would also have known, as Anzieu points out, that "the bird-headed Egyptian god, Thoth, is pronounced in German the same way as *Tot* (the German word for 'a dead person')" (1986: 300). The Deuteronomic text itself warns against forbidden deities upon the threat of death:

> Beware lest you act corruptly by making a graven image for yourselves, in the form of any figure . . . the likeness of any winged bird that flies in the air. . . . If you act corruptly by making a graven image . . . you will soon utterly perish from the land . . . you will not live long upon it but will be utterly destroyed . . . you will serve gods of wood and stone. (Deut. 4:16–28)

The presence of foreign gods whose worship presages death thus stands in for the absence of the "true" God.[21]

Even the location of this dream in *The Interpretation of Dreams* underscores its association with death and immortality. The dream of the bird-beaked figures is the last dream Freud presents in the "dream book." Just as his final words in "A Religious Experience" reiterate the finality of death and the "immortality" of psychoanalytic interpretation, Freud's final dream analysis in this book gives him the last word on death: he attempts to subsume death through words of interpretation and analysis. Anzieu's remarks support my conclusion:

> By placing the interpretation of [this] dream at the end of his book, he was confirming that he had taken back his beloved mother from his father and regained possession of her; but, more than that, he was indicating that he now had the last word on death, the last word on anxiety, the last word on separation from the primally loved object. For death, anxiety and separation are inevitable facts of life which we can counter (indeed, only counter) with words. (Anzieu 1986: 309)[22]

A careful reading of Freud's texts exposes numerous such analyses. We find that death anxieties and misogynist fears will accompany social and religious change, notions of a heavenly afterlife, and anti-Semitic encounters with the "Other." These analyses, in which misogyny and death anxiety are intertwined with but cannot be reduced to castration anxiety, are not woven into a coherent theory, nor can they be smoothly integrated into Freud's Oedipal paradigm. They provide traces of the counterthesis from which he repeatedly turned away.

CHAPTER 2

Death, Mothers, and the Afterlife

At Home in the Uncanny

One of the sites at which the counterthesis emerges most clearly is the site of death, the site of the fears and fantasies surrounding mortality. Freud's interpretation of death is generally seen as supportive of the Oedipal master thesis which shaped so much of his work. Cultural theorist Peter Homans, for example, asserts, "In Freud's mature psychoanalytic theory, death was ... a drive which polarized around the father" (1989: 98). Death wishes toward the father and fears of paternal retribution, Freud often argued, shape all human relationships with the authorities of culture, state, religion, and family: in psychoanalytic theory, parricide is both universal fantasy and primal deed. In both *The Ego and the Id* and "The Economic Problem of Masochism," Freud describes humankind's "realistic fear of death" as a fear of retribution and punishment by an Oedipal parent (*SE* 19: 58, 168). Destiny and fate are similarly understood within an Oedipal framework: "Even Fate," Freud remarks, "is in the last resort, only a later projection of the father" (*SE* 21: 185).

A number of texts within the Freudian corpus, however, tell a very different story, a story in which death is associated with the usually "beloved," idealized, and eroticized mother, a story in which immortality and the afterlife are associated with the maternal (*SE* 5: 583; *SE* 21:

113). While a massive accumulation of literature on Freud and religion has been produced in recent decades, little attention has been directed to Freud's analyses of the religious consolation in the ideas of immortality and the afterlife. And few theorists have noted the gendering of death, destiny, immortality, and the afterlife in this virtually unexamined territory within Freud's psychology of religion.[1] An examination of these themes provides a rough cartography of that uncharted terrain.

Three kinds of images are associated with immortality and the afterlife in Freud's writings: images of dead mothers, images of mothers as instructors in death, and images of "uncanny" maternal bodies. As I noted earlier, my interest in pursuing this material is not motivated by a desire to dismiss Freud's work for its internal contradictions. This material constitutes elements of a counterthesis challenging the Oedipal theory and embodying a set of observations undeveloped but potentially significant for the psychoanalytic theory of religion. Nor is my interest in exposing this counterthesis motivated by a desire to attack Freud for what might be considered his veiled misogyny. We can benefit, as I suggested above, from close attention not only to the Oedipal interpretation of the construction of gender in patriarchal culture, but also to the linkages of maternity, mortality, and immortality in Freud's incompletely developed non-Oedipal counterthesis.

From the perspective of psychoanalytic theory, fantasies are "obscure revelations of . . . the truth of unconscious psychical activity . . . openings into a hidden world of 'psychic reality.'" Freud's aim was to "excavate the inner history of psychosexual desire through an interpretation of the signs — images, gestures, words, symptomatic actions — through which this desire both revealed and hid itself" (Toews 1991: 513). In Freud's texts, such "signs" — images of mothers, immortality, and the afterlife — and interpretations can be interrogated as openings into widespread, although seldom acknowledged "psychic realities" in which misogyny, matriphobia, and matricide lie in close proximity to fantasies of immortality and the afterlife.

THE BODY IN THE TEXT:
REVISITING THE DEAD MOTHER

The most visible trace of the counterthesis linking mortality, immortality, and the mother is the body in the text: bodies of dead mothers appear throughout Freud's writings. We saw in chapter 1 two sites of the maternal corpse in the Freudian corpus: Freud's short text "A Religious Experience" and a childhood dream of a dead mother. Here we pursue this trajectory further, examining a chapter from *Beyond the Pleasure Principle* and the provocative essay "Medusa's Head." At these sites, as in "A Religious Experience" and the childhood dream, a dead or deadly mother is central; God, immortality, and the afterlife are prominent; and the presence of the dead mother once again is paradoxically denied.

In the famous story near the beginning of *Beyond the Pleasure Principle,* the text that introduced the controversial notion of the "death drive," Freud recounts in the text and footnotes a poignant story of a dead mother. The story involves a child's first game, the game of *fort* and *da*. A child one and one-half years of age, Freud recounts, repeatedly threw a toy across the room exclaiming "o-o-o," which Freud interpreted as *fort*, the German word for "gone." The child greeted the return of the toy with the exclamation "a-a-a," or *da* ("there"). In Freud's analysis, this game of "disappearance and return" was a manifestation of the child's mastery of anxiety over maternal absence, an expression of the child's "great cultural achievement, the instinctual renunciation . . . in allowing his mother to go away without protesting" (*SE* 18: 15). The game, in other words, revealed the child's ability to tolerate the absence of the mother and the delay of gratification while awaiting the mother's return.

Not only does the game of disappearance and return inspired by maternal absence thus emerge as a metaphor for the experience of loss and recovery and for the postponement of gratification, in addition, in

Freud's text, it becomes a metaphor for life and death. In a footnote, Freud informs the reader that "when this child was five-and-three-quarters, his mother died" (*SE* 18: 16 n. 1). Her temporary absence was replaced by the permanent absence of death. This striking story gains additional force from its biographical and autobiographical context, which is absent from Freud's text. The mother, first temporarily, then permanently absent, was Freud's twenty-six-year-old daughter Sophie, mother of two young boys and pregnant with a third child at the time of her death in 1920. Young Ernst, Sophie's elder son and the inventor of the game of *fort* and *da,* Freud noted, "showed no signs of grief" at her death (16 n. 1). But Freud himself, we know from other sources, mourned deeply. His letters speak eloquently of his grief at the death of the mother/daughter Sophie. He described his reaction to the "paralyzing event" in terms of "blunt necessity, mute submission" (Jones 1957: 20). He wrote to his colleague Ferenczi: "Since I am profoundly irreligious there is no one I can accuse and I know there is nowhere to which any complaint could be addressed" (Jones 1957: 20–21). In these private reflections on Sophie's death, the absence of God is palpable. To borrow a phrase from Peter Homans which we will encounter again below, "Freud was able to add the idea of God only by way of negation" (1989: 99).

Concerned lest his colleagues conclude that Sophie's death was related to the notion of the death drive in *Beyond the Pleasure Principle* published in the same year, Freud took pains to point out that the text was "written in 1919 when my daughter was young and blooming" (Jones 1957: 43). I have no quarrel with Freud's insistence that his development of the idea of a death drive preceded Sophie's death. What interests me, however, is that he chose to introduce this particular text with an account of maternal absence and maternal mortality. *Beyond the Pleasure Principle* reframes the psychoanalytic masterplot by speculating that death is precisely *not* the "drive which polarized around the father" described by Homans (98). The death drive or death instinct in *Beyond the Pleasure Principle* is instead a physiological, biological, or cellular

"pulsion" toward death, a physical drive with psychological manifestations in the "repetition compulsion," a drive with connections to maternal presence and absence. "By unwittingly demonstrating the interplay
between symbolization and maternal absence," Elizabeth Bronfen
notes, *"Beyond the Pleasure Principle* contain[s] a narrative about the
relationship between culturation and death" (Bronfen 1992: 19). In
Freud's account, this drive toward death, which can take the form of a
drive to return to one's origins, is a consistent trajectory toward decreas-
ing tension, seeking the ultimate cessation of all tension and stimuli in
death: "The aim of all life is death" (*SE* 18: 38). The story of the
absent/dead mother and the child's game establish a structure which is
reenacted in the theoretical argument of the text: maternal absence/
death and the alternating *da* and *fort* of the child's game provide the
foundation and paradigm for the drive toward death theorized by
Freud.

This text initiated by a dead mother/daughter is not only a text about
death. It is also about immortality and, at least rhetorically, about the
afterlife. Some definitions might clarify the distinction between the two
terms. The notion of immortality for Freud involves the escape from
death by living forever: Freud's term is *Unsterblichkeit,* which might be
literally translated "nondeath" or "undeath." According to Freud, the
belief in one's own immortality, *Unsterblichkeit,* is an unconscious con-
stant: "It is true that the statement 'all men are mortal' is paraded in
textbooks of logic as an example of a general proposition, but no human
being ever really grasps it and our unconscious has as little use now as it
ever had for the idea of its own mortality" (*SE* 17: 242). The notion of
an afterlife, on the other hand, implies a heavenly existence following
death. The term Freud most often uses, *Jenseits,* means "the other side,"
the "hereafter," the "beyond," or the "other world." It is, in Freud's
view, a common fantasy, embellished by religions worldwide.

The issue of immortality has proven to be one of the most trouble-
some elements of *Beyond the Pleasure Principle* for its interpreters
(Becker 1973, Boothby 1991, Brown 1959, Laplanche 1976). The text, in

a sense, refuses to hold to its own thesis. If the central point of *Beyond the Pleasure Principle* is that the final aim of life is death and that life can be described as "circuitous paths to death" (*SE* 18: 39), Freud explicitly undercut his own argument with a chapter on immortality added after the bulk of the manuscript was complete (Jones 1957: 43). This chapter describes scientific research on protozoa which, Freud indicated, may be proof of the immortality of single-celled organisms: "Germ cells are potentially immortal ... death only makes its appearance with the multicellular metazoa" (*SE* 18: 46). Immortality, in other words, interrupts the argument of this text on mortality.

The afterlife figures prominently here, as well, if only in linguistic play. The title of this text in German is *Jenseits des Lustprinzips,* literally *The Hereafter of the Pleasure Principle.* According to David Bakan and Ernest Jones, Freud often referred to this book in English as *The Hereafter* and in German as *Jenseits* (Bakan 1966: 178; Jones 1957: 43). A 1923 letter to his colleague and biographer Fritz Wittels brings together the entire set of ideas expressive of the counterthesis: the idea of the hereafter, the notion of immortality, and the question of the significance of Sophie's death in the development of the ideas in the book. Freud writes, "I certainly would have stressed the connection between the death of the daughter and the concepts of *The Hereafter* in any analytic study on someone else. Yet it is still wrong. *The Hereafter* was written in 1919 ... it lacked ... only the part on mortality or immortality of the protozoa" (Jones 1957: 43). A daughter (who is also a mother) is brought into the same metaphorical and rhetorical frame as death, immortality, and the afterlife in the context of a negation or denial.[2]

A text composed contemporaneously with *Beyond the Pleasure Principle* that we'll discuss below, "The Uncanny," also exhibits this slippage from death to the afterlife and from mortality to immortality. There, Freud wrote:

> Biology has not yet been able to deduce whether death is the inevitable fate of every living being or whether it is only a regular but

yet perhaps avoidable event in life . . . our unconscious has as little use now as ever for the idea of its own mortality. Religions continue to dispute the undeniable fact of the death of each one of us and to postulate a life after death. (Freud, *CP* 4: 395)

As we shall see, Freud's analysis of the experience of the uncanny in the encounter with death is closely related to an experience of the uncanny evoked by the body of the mother.[3]

Both *Beyond the Pleasure Principle* and "The Uncanny" contain three theses regarding death, immortality, and the afterlife: there is an internal drive toward death; immortality may truly exist; and the hereafter *(Jenseits)* has at least a linguistic reality. This complex set of communications about death, immortality, and the afterlife is introduced by a mother whose absence taught her young son to play a game of presence and absence and whose death gives the narrative a chilling turn. *Beyond the Pleasure Principle* underscores the connections hinted at in chapter 1 in my discussion of "A Religious Experience" and the dream of the beaked birds: the dead body of the mother lies within the same plot as the fantasy of immortality and the afterlife. The plot of *Beyond the Pleasure Principle* differs substantially from the Oedipal masterplot within which the father is interred.

Another paradigmatic text exhibiting the theme of the dead/deadly mother is "Medusa's Head," an essay Freud refused to publish during his lifetime. Written in 1922, it was published posthumously in 1940. A sketchy outline for an analysis, rather than a full interpretation, this text provides a concise example of the tension between masterplot and counterthesis.

Freud begins "Medusa's Head" with an uncomplicated account of castration anxiety as the source of the myth of Medusa along the lines of the Oedipal masterplot, even using the mathematical symbol for equivalence in his sentence: "An interpretation suggests itself easily in the case of the horrifying decapitated head of Medusa. To decapitate = to castrate" (*SE* 18: 273). But this is not a simple castrative equation. The myth involves a terrifying head which cannot be looked at directly and whose source, Freud proposes, is the "horrifying" maternal genitals. Elements of the counterthesis — the maternal body, female deities, and death — thus begin to emerge. Freud speculates about the source of the castration anxiety: a boy "catches sight of the female genitals, probably those of an adult, surrounded by hair, and essentially those of his mother" (273). He traces the mythic linkage of the horrifying Medusa with the goddess Athene, noting the appropriateness of the symbolism: "This symbol of horror (*Grauen*) is worn upon her dress by the virgin goddess Athene. And rightly so, for thus she becomes a woman who is unapproachable and repels all sexual desires — since she displays the terrifying genitals of the Mother" (273–74).

Like the triple goddess in "The Theme of the Three Caskets," whom we'll encounter in the next section of this chapter, this double goddess Medusa-Athene brings death. Paralysis, petrification, or rigor mortis are the punishments for looking at the Medusa face to face. But in the reversal that Freud so often enacts, the stiffening of death is transformed into a different stiffening, a stiffening signaling male sexual desire: the erection. Death is transmuted into sex: "The sight of Medusa's head makes the spectator stiff with terror, turns him to stone . . . becoming stiff means an erection . . . he is still in possession of a penis, and the stiffening reassures him of the fact" (*SE* 18: 273). God the father is absent, replaced here by the presence of two unapproachable and deadly goddesses, a virgin and a mother, and in a comparative analysis on the following page, by "the Devil," who "took to flight" at the sight of a woman's vulva in Rabelais (274). The theme of homosexuality emerges here, as well, although quite briefly: "Since the Greeks were in the main strongly homosexual, it was inevitable that we should find among them a representation of woman as a being who frightens and repels because she is castrated" (274).[4]

The dead mother whose corpse we have found haunting many of Freud's texts is, of course, the Medusa herself in this essay. Freud does not remind the reader of the myth in which the heroic Perseus finally succeeds in killing (decapitating) the Medusa by gazing not directly at

her face, but at her reflection in his shield. But he reenacts Perseus's gesture himself by looking away from his analysis of the Medusa in a kind
of textual mirrored reversal. After describing the horror underlying the
Greek myth of Medusa's head and Rabelais's reiteration of the motif, he
himself turns aside, looking away to examine "another mechanism," a
mirrored reversal of the threatening/castrated maternal genitals: "The
erect male organ also has an apotropaic effect" (274), he insists. "To display the penis or any of its surrogates is to say: 'I am not afraid of you. I
defy you. I have a penis.'" And he concludes with a negated reference to
God: "Here then is another way of intimidating the Evil Spirit" (274).
In Freud's text equivalence (" = ") thus gives way to equivocation.

This text is exemplary of both masterplot and counterthesis. In the
body of the text, Freud interpreted the "horrifying" associations of
maternal genitals, female deities, and death (the counterthesis). Yet he
concluded his argument with an insistent return to the safety of the
"erect male organ" (the Oedipal masterplot). He broke off his analysis
as if he could not come "face to face," like Perseus before the Medusa,
with the implications of his interpretation, just as he turned away at the
"navel of the dream" discussed in chapter 1. And his refusal to publish
the text during his lifetime expresses yet again his resistance to the
counterthesis.

In spite of his resistance to publishing his analysis of Medusa's head,
Freud commented briefly on the same subject in a published essay,
"Infantile Genital Organization," written in 1923, shortly after he composed "Medusa." There, in an analysis of the source of misogyny and
homosexuality in castration anxiety ("We know, too, to what a degree
depreciation of women, horror of women, and a disposition to homosexuality are derived from the final conviction that women have no
penis"), he credited his colleague Ferenczi with the initial insight that
the myth of Medusa refers to the horror of the female genitals.
"Ferenczi has recently, with complete justice, traced back the mytho-
logical symbol of horror — Medusa's head — to the impression of the
female genitals devoid of a penis" (*SE* 19: 144). Freud added the insight

fundamental to the unpublished text, speculating, in a footnote, that the horror is specifically related to the *mother's* genitals: "I should like to add that what is indicated in the myth is the mother's genitals. Athene, who carries Medusa's head on her armour, becomes in consequence, the unapproachable woman, the sight of whom extinguishes all thought of a sexual approach" (144 n. 3).

While these published remarks reiterate many of the same points as the essay that remained unpublished until after Freud's death, they are far briefer than even the brief text "Medusa's Head." They lack the subtle references to death and deities present in the "Medusa," they dissociate the original insight from Freud, crediting Ferenczi instead, and they bury the reference to the mother in a footnote. The published remarks focus almost entirely on sex: in a repetition of the gesture emblematic of his resistance to developing the counterthesis, Freud replaced death with sex. His publication of the mere skeleton of the argument in "Infantile Genital Organization," by replacing death, deities, and immortality with a simple story of sex, highlights that resistance. His foray into the terrain of the counterthesis, evident in the posthumously published text, is clearly visible, but remains partial, hesitant, and deferred.

A PEDAGOGY OF MORTALITY

Maternity and mortality appear in another guise in Freud's texts: the mother, to use another of Peter Homans's terms, is the "instructress in mortality" (1989: 98), the master teacher in a pedagogy of death. We'll encounter this image twice, first in a dream of Freud's often called the "dream of the three Fates" (Anzieu 1986: 362; Erikson 1964: 178; Grinstein 1968: 161), and second in "The Theme of the Three Caskets."

"Tired and hungry after a journey," Freud recounted in *The Interpretation of Dreams,*

> I went to bed. I dreamt as follows: I went into a kitchen in search of some pudding. Three women were standing in it; one of them was

the hostess of the inn and was twisting something about in her hand, as though she was making *Knödel* [dumplings]. She answered that I must wait till she was ready. . . . I felt impatient and went off with a sense of injury. (*SE* 4: 204)

Freud's association to this dream of three women centers upon the mythic figures of the three Fates: "In connection with the three women I thought of the three Fates who spin the destiny of man." The third of the Fates, rubbing her palms together, evoked a memory from childhood in which Freud had learned of death literally at the hands of his mother.

When I was six years old and was given my first lessons by my mother, I was expected to believe that we were all made of earth and must therefore return to earth. This did not suit me and I expressed doubts of the doctrine. My mother thereupon rubbed the palms of her hands together — just as she did in making dumplings, except that there was no dough between them — and showed me the blackish scales of epidermis produced by the friction as a proof that we were made of earth.

"So they really were Fates that I found in the kitchen when I went into it," Freud reflected, "as I had so often done in my childhood when I was hungry, while my mother, standing by the fire, had admonished me that I must wait till dinner was ready" (205).

In the dream of the three Fates and the memory of the first lesson, awareness of death was thus associated "not only with a mother, but with a mother who was withholding food" (Homans 1989: 99). Insisting on a delay in oral gratification, she demanded that he wait. The dream of the three Fates casts the mother in the role of educator who teaches the son to defer his desires by insisting on a delay before he can appease his hunger. This maternal law is not the forbidding "*nom* (or *non*)-*du-père*" described by Lacan (1977: xi). Rather than the paternal "No!" what the mother teaches is "Not yet!" Like the absent mother in *Beyond the Pleasure Principle,* she teaches children the "great cultural achievement" in the heroic gesture of delay: the toleration of maternal absence, the ability to wait, hungry, for the mother's return. But the sense of injury generated by the enforced delay is equivalent, in a sense, to the wound dealt by death: this figure twisting dough in her hands also teaches the necessity of death. She is the mother demonstrating "that we are made of earth," and she is the "third of the Fates," who cuts the thread of human life. In Sarah Kofman's words, she is "a figure of necessity . . . the one who silently teaches her child to resign himself to the inevitable, unacceptable, and stupefying necessity of Death" (1985: 74).

The imagery of epidermis and the dough as evidence of death reappears in another text. In *Beyond the Pleasure Principle,* Freud describes a "dead layer" or "crust . . . 'baked through' . . . a shield against stimuli" (*SE* 18: 26–27) which protects living inner layers of living cells from excessive stimulation: "By its death the outer layer has saved all the deeper ones from a similar fate" (*SE* 18: 27). Skin, crust, or dough thus serve as images of death, each associated with the handwork of women. The lessons at the hands of the mother involve waiting to eat and waiting to die.

In this maternal pedagogy of delay and death, ideas about immortality and the afterlife are ubiquitous, as are ideas about the presence and absence of God. Having been shown the "blackish scales of epidermis" between his mother's hands as proof of the inevitability of death, Freud recounts, he finally "acquiesced in the belief which [he] was later to hear expressed in the words: '*Du bist der Natur einen Tod schuldig*' [Thou owest Nature a death]" (*SE* 4: 205). The quote within the quote is from Shakespeare, but significantly, it is a misquotation. Shakespeare's line is "Thou owest God a death" (*SE* 4: 205 n. 2). Freud thus substituted "Nature" for "God." In Homans's reading, Freud's parapraxis regarding Shakespeare's line is an explicit reference to and negation of God: "To the linkage, mother/awareness of death, Freud was able to add the idea of God only by way of negation, for 'God' and 'nature' are, in the history of Western thought, negatives of each other" (99).[5]

Other interpreters of this dream and Freud's associations to it have drawn conclusions which parallel mine. Erik Erikson, for example, notes that Freud replaces God with women and with death: "The associating dreamer thus puts nature, that is, a maternal figure, in the place of God, implying that a pact with maternal women is a pact — with death" (182). And Ana Maria Rizzuto, noting that Freud "linked his mother to death" (1998: 238), states that Freud's misquotation "strongly suggests the unconscious representational admixing in his mind of mother, nature, and God" (238).[6]

Elsewhere, as well, Freud explicitly linked the experience of postponed gratification with belief in the afterlife:

> A momentary pleasure, uncertain in its results, is given up, but only in order to gain along the new path an assured pleasure at a later time. But the endopsychic impression made by this substitution has been so powerful that it is reflected in a special religious myth. The doctrine of reward in the afterlife for the — voluntary or enforced — renunciation of earthly pleasures is nothing other than a mythical projection of this revolution in the mind. (*SE* 12: 223)

In this text, an ungendered postponement is the experience generating the notion of reward in the afterlife. In the dream of the three Fates and the memory of epidermis and dumplings, the renunciatory wait demanded by the reality principle is the particular message of maternal pedagogy, the mark of the mother.

While the mother is literally the instructress in mortality in the dream of the three Fates and in Freud's childhood memory, the short essay "The Theme of the Three Caskets" transforms the mother into death itself. Freud described the motif, widespread in folktale, literature, and myth, of a hero who, faced with a choice among three caskets, must select the correct casket in order to win a bride, knowing that the wrong choice will win him death. Tracing a double reversal of destiny, Freud shows that since death is our final destiny, the myths give the hero a choice where no choice actually exists, transforming destiny's "gift" into its opposite. The first move is a transformation of death into love: the "imagination rebelled against the recognition of the truth . . . and constructed instead the myth . . . in which the Goddess of Death was replaced by the Goddess of Love" (*SE* 12: 299). The second move transforms destiny into choice: "Here again there has been a wishful reversal. Choice stands in the place of necessity, of destiny. In this way man overcomes death, which he has recognized intellectually. No greater triumph of wish-fulfillment is conceivable. A choice is made, where in reality there is obedience to a compulsion and what is chosen is not a figure of terror but the fairest and most desirable of women" (299).

The three women in these myths, Freud wrote, "are the three inevitable relations that a man has with a woman — the woman who bears him, the woman who is his mate, and the woman who destroys him." Freud described the three women as "the three forms taken by the figure of the mother in the course of a man's life — the mother herself, the beloved one who is chosen after her pattern, and lastly, the Mother Earth who receives him once more" (301). "The Theme of the Three Caskets" thus links mother and lover with the Goddess of Death and inverts the fear of death in male fantasies of selecting a bride and returning to the arms of the mother.[7] Death loses its terror through reversal in myths of sexual union and maternal embrace. But these reversals have a double edge: the maternal is also fearful and terrifying; maternal embrace and sexual union become dangerous embodiments of or disguises for death. Here the woman is not only a dead mother: "She may be something else as well. Namely, Death itself, the Goddess of Death" (*SE* 12: 296). Freud's final words in this essay reiterate this entanglement of mothers and death: "It is in vain that an old man yearns for the love of woman as he had it first from his mother; the third of the Fates alone, the silent Goddess of Death will take him into her arms" (301). What seems to be a mother or a bride is really "the silent Goddess of Death." Eros becomes Thanatos, presence becomes absence, and mothers become death. A mythic account of love and choice is exposed as a complex and highly ambiguous attempt both to escape from death and to embrace death as one embraces a mother.[8]

Kofman finds in this text a typical and troubling "double gesture," a fragmented description of maternal omnipotence as Great Goddess which is quickly redefined and defanged, as it were, within a domesticated framework. "This double gesture on Freud's part," she writes, "turns up everywhere: on the one hand, the acknowledgment of the (fantasmatic) maternal omnipotence transformed into a Fate or a great goddess; on the other hand, a dream of turning this power to the profit of man" (Kofman 1985: 80). I disagree with Kofman's interpretation. Freud is not simply a misogynist here: I find in this "double gesture" an indication of masterplot and counterthesis in tension. A broader view incorporating the counterthesis enables us to perceive Freud's complex, although incomplete efforts at cultural analysis in this "double gesture."

An erasure of God lies within this double gesture as well. The paternal deity of the Western religious tradition has become a maternal deity, and his role as creator and protector of life is displaced by her role as Goddess of Death. Like the dead mother and the denial of the afterlife, which evoked an overwhelming feeling of the absence of God in the American doctor discussed in chapter 1, this Mother Goddess whose responsibility is death stands for the absence of the Father God in the text. While in the interpretations of his own dream of the dying mother and the American doctor's crisis of faith Freud had replaced anxiety over maternal death with incestuous sexual anxiety, this essay directly addresses the displacement of death by sex. Describing the displacement in myth and literature, Freud interprets it. In this text, Max Schur argues, "Freud met the theme of death head-on, perhaps for the first time" (1972: 274). In my view, Schur is too cautious. This was not only one of Freud's "first" direct textual engagements with death, it was one of his few direct textual encounters with death other than his writings on the death drive. Freud's open engagement with the imagery of death and the mother in this text stands as an anomaly in relation to his other writings, which typically allow these concepts to emerge only in fragments.

In his more typical Oedipal analyses, Freud maintained that every punishment in life, every mishap or disappointment, is experienced as an Oedipal castration. Every punishment "is ultimately castration, and as such, a fulfillment of the old passive attitude towards the father" (*SE* 21: 185). He reiterated this thought more than once: "It seems very hard to free oneself" from a "parental view of fate" (*SE* 19: 168). Freud saw himself, however, as one who had succeeded in the difficult task of transcending this Oedipal relation to fate, one of the few who are capable of encountering fate or destiny without projecting unconscious familial patterns: "The last figure in the series that began with the parents is the dark power of Destiny which only the fewest of us are able to look upon as impersonal" (*SE* 19: 168). He argues that

> there is little to be said against the Dutch writer Multatuli when he replaces the *Moira* (Destiny) of the Greeks by the divine pair *Logos kai Ananke* (Reason and Necessity); but all who transfer the guidance of the world to Providence, to God, or to God and Nature, arouse a suspicion that they still look upon these ultimate and remotest powers as a parental couple in a mythological sense and believe themselves linked to them by libidinal ties. (*SE* 19: 168)

Most of us, in other words, encounter the exigencies of destiny as punishments of an Oedipal, castrating father. Freud suggested that he and other superior thinkers escape the "passive attitude toward the father" where fate is a father projection (*SE* 21: 185). But Freud's counterthesis suggests that fate or destiny sometimes takes another, quite different parental form. In "The Theme of the Three Caskets" and the dream of the three Fates, where the counterthesis emerges with clarity, the third of the fates, both mother and death, will "take us into her arms." These texts suggest that the mother is a figure whose embrace is simultaneously nurturant, erotic, and deadly. Freud comes close in these texts to an open acknowledgment of a longing for the mother which is intertwined with a misogynist fear of her, a desire for death which is intertwined with a fear of it, and an acknowledgment of an affiliation between mortal mothers, the absence of God, and the fantasy of immortality.[9]

This complex set of intertwined fears and fantasies is not uncommon in contemporary culture. I see it as a widespread, although virtually unacknowledged, "psychic reality," which, precisely because it remains unacknowledged, continues to produce emotional, social, and cultural damage in the lives of men and women alike.

AN UNCANNY HOME AND A HOME IN THE UNCANNY: THE MOTHER'S BODY AND THE AFTERLIFE

Freud's texts "The Uncanny" and *The Future of an Illusion* contain further evidence of an attempt to analyze this set of intertwined fears and fantasies. These texts present a set of images linking the maternal body and the afterlife through a common association with the uncanny. They also move hesitantly toward an interpretation of these images and their interconnections.

The essay "The Uncanny" ("Das Unheimliche"), published shortly before *Beyond the Pleasure Principle* and "set against a background of war, death, the death instinct" (Kofman 1991: 123), illustrates with particular clarity Freud's two theses in tension: an Oedipal master plot persistently interrupted and undercut by a non-Oedipal counterthesis. Many theorists have pointed out contradictions in the structure and development of "The Uncanny." Hélène Cixous, for example, describes the "text and its hesitating shadow," noting that "what is brought together here is quickly undone, what asserts itself becomes suspect; each thread leads to its net or to some kind of disentanglement" (1976: 525).

In "The Uncanny," Freud explored the realm of the experiences that arouse dread and horror. He offered a linguistic analysis of the term "uncanny," an interpretation of a story, "The Sand-Man," by E. T. A. Hoffmann, a "collection of examples" further illustrating the feeling of the uncanny (*SE* 17: 245), and a metapsychological analysis of the source of this feeling. Freud's linguistic analysis of the uncanny reveals the ambiguity of the word itself. While the word *unheimlich* means "strange" and "uncanny," the word *heimlich* can refer to either the familiar and agreeable or to what is hidden, concealed, kept out of sight, unfamiliar, and strange: "Among its different shades of meaning, the word '*heimlich*' exhibits one which is identical with its opposite, '*unheimlich*'. What is *heimlich* thus comes to be *unheimlich* . . . everything is *unheimlich* that ought to have remained secret and hidden but has come to light" (224–25). He explains further that what is *heimlich* "develops in the direction of ambivalence until it finally coincides with its opposite, *unheimlich*" (226).

This linguistic analysis establishes the foundation for Freud's interpretation of Hoffmann's "Sand-Man" and other sites of the uncanny. The linguistic ambivalence of the word, he argues, echoes a psychological ambivalence. Long-abandoned ideas which reemerge after having been repressed will generate a sense of the uncanny: "We can understand why linguistic usage has extended *das Heimliche* . . . into its opposite, *das Unheimliche;* for this uncanny is in reality nothing new or alien, but something which is familiar and old-established in the mind and which has become alienated from it only through the process of repression" (*SE* 17: 241). These long-abandoned ideas, however, are quite specific. The dominant thesis Freud develops and pursues is that the uncanny emerges from the return of repressed castration fears. Interrupting this thesis is a counterthesis in which the uncanny emerges from the return of repressed ideas associating death, the mother, and immortality.

Hoffmann's tale "The Sand-Man," a central piece of Freud's analysis of the uncanny, is a complex story involving a young man's childhood memories and fears, his love for two young women, his conflicts with father figures, and his insanity and suicide. Three central moments of the story stand out in Freud's retelling and interpretation.

First, a set of childhood memories: as a child, the young Nathaniel was occasionally sent to bed early after being told by his mother that the "Sand-Man" was coming. His nurse explained that this wicked man would throw sand into the eyes of children who refuse to go to bed, steal their bleeding eyes, and feed the eyes to his own bird-children who would use their hooked, owl-like beaks to peck and eat the eyes of the naughty boys and girls (*SE* 17: 228). Undeterred by these warnings and determined to observe the Sand-Man, Nathaniel hid in his father's study one night. He saw his father working with a guest, Coppelius, at a brazier with glowing flames. The child heard Coppelius call out: "Eyes here! Eyes here!" (228). He screamed aloud, revealing his presence. Coppelius attempted to burn the child's eyes, but he was saved by his father. The trauma led to a long illness for the child. A year later, an explosion killed Nathaniel's father while he was again working in his study with Coppelius.

In the second major narrative moment, Nathaniel, now an older student, sees a double of Coppelius — "Coppola" — selling spyglasses or spectacles. He buys one, and while using it, sees through a window a beautiful, but silent woman, Olympia, with whom he falls violently and obsessively in love. Olympia, he later discovers, is an automaton created by her "father" and Coppola. A struggle ensues between Nathaniel and Olympia's creators, during which her eyes fall out. Coppola carries off the eyeless, wooden doll. The "father" picks up Olympia's bleeding eyes from the ground and throws them at Nathaniel, saying that Coppola had stolen them from the student. Nathaniel "succumbs to a fresh attack of madness" (229). Crying out "spin about, ring of fire . . . wooden doll, spin about," Nathaniel tries to strangle Olympia's "father."

In the third central moment, having recovered from madness, Nathaniel is engaged to Clara, a clever and sensible young woman. They climb the high tower of the town hall. Looking through Coppola's spyglass, he falls into a new attack of madness. Crying out "Ring of fire, spin about!" he attempts to throw Clara from the tower. Rescued by her brother, Clara descends, while Nathaniel, having caught sight of Coppelius/Coppola, shrieks "fine eyes, fine eyes," and flings himself over the parapet to his death. Freud ends his summary of the narrative with the words "While he lies on the paving stones with a shattered skull, the Sand-Man vanishes in the throng" (230).

Freud's interpretation emphasizes Oedipal and castrative themes. The "arbitrary and meaningless" elements in the story, he argues, "become intelligible as soon as we replace the Sand-Man by the dreaded father at whose hands castration is expected" (232). He emphasizes the castration anxiety underlying the fear of blindness, recalling Oedipus's self-punishment: "Anxiety about one's eyes, the fear of going blind, is often enough a substitute for the dread of being castrated. The self-blinding of the mythical criminal, Oedipus, was simply a mitigated form of the punishment of castration — the only punishment that was adequate for him by the *lex talionis*" (231). The Sand-Man, in Freud's view, generates a feeling of uncanniness because of the return of the repressed castration complex: "We shall venture therefore to refer the uncanny effect of the Sand-Man to the anxiety belonging to the castration complex of childhood" (233).

Alongside his castrative theory, Freud presents, but rejects, an alternative interpretation. He describes an analysis of the story and its uncanniness by a turn-of-the-century theorist, E. Jentsch, in which the uncanny is said to depend on the "intellectual uncertainty" over whether an object is alive or not, an uncertainty emerging "when an inanimate object becomes too much like an animate one" (233). Acknowledging that the ambiguous qualities of the doll/woman Olympia — alive and not alive, animate and inanimate — would seem to support Jentsch's view, he nevertheless argues that this ambiguity plays a negligible role in evoking the uncanny effect: "Jentsch's point of an intellectual uncertainty has nothing to do with the effect. Uncertainty whether an object is living or inanimate, which admittedly applied to the doll Olympia, is quite irrelevant in connection with this other more striking instance of uncanniness" (230).

Freud's rationale for dismissing the living/inanimate Olympia as the source of the uncanniness in the story is simply that the Sand-Man is the dominant and titular theme. The Sand-Man and the fear of castration, he claims, are the true source of the sense of uncanniness because Hoffmann's title suggests that the Sand-Man is the central focus: "The main theme of the story is . . . something which gives it its name and which is always reintroduced at critical moments: it is the theme of the "Sand-Man who tears out children's eyes" (227). He argues further that the author's satiric treatment of the hero's relationship to Olympia militates against attributing uncanniness to Olympia. Yet after challenging Jentsch's theory early in the essay, he returns to it again and again (227, 230, 233), as if he cannot quite dismiss it. Death, or the theme of the living/dead, animate/inanimate woman, rather than castration, seems to demand centrality.

Here, as in so many texts, Freud insists that castration anxiety is the foundational anxiety and that death anxiety is a secondary phenomenon, yet the priority of death over castration is irrepressibly expressed through textual interruptions and inconsistencies. "Everything takes place as if Freud could not bear the importance of his discovery concerning the death instincts and as if 'The Uncanny' with its successive invalidations, its tortuous procedure, is a last effort to conceal 'the [real] return of the repressed [death]'" (Kofman 1991: 160).[10]

Freud's essay thus documents a hesitant exploration of — and resistance to — the themes of the counterthesis. His compulsive returns to Jentsch's thesis represent tentative forays into the terrain where mortality, immortality, and the mother are intertwined with the uncanny. The deadly mother, present in the other texts we have examined, is obscured in this text — yet her spectral presence has not been erased entirely. The Sand-Man has deadly maternal qualities: he tears out children's eyes as food for his own little children, a hint that the story itself can be read as a fantasy concealing the fear of death at the hands of a dangerous mother. This is a story in which the mother's presence is so frightening that she is negated. Hoffmann's tale contains two central accounts of motherless procreation. The events witnessed by Nathaniel as a child

enacted a distorted "primal scene." And the student's encounter with
the two "fathers" of Olympia provide a structural reminder of that
early, motherless act of reproduction. The acts of creation occur
between two men, providing a hint of the theme of homosexuality. The
"primal scene" transpires at night, in private. Specific sounds are associated with it: thudding of steps coming up the stairs and "characteristic creakings" (Kofman 1991: 149). Mothers are excluded from this act
of creation, while the father, playing the childbearing role, dies in an
"explosion" which reenacts and transforms a fantasy of maternal death
in childbirth. ·

In Freud's negation of the mother, in his giving the father the role of
dead mother and presenting obliquely a "maternal" or nurturant figure
associated with death through an image we encountered in the previous
chapter, bird beaks, we encounter the foundational themes of the
uncanny: death and the mother. "What seems to be unbearable and
unheimlich is this identification with the mother and the death which
she threatens; this internalization of the forbidden mother, who can be
considered an analogon of the death instincts" (Kofman 1991: 162).

The sequence and development of Freud's subsequent argument in
"The Uncanny," after his discussion of "The Sand-Man," repeats his
earlier pattern of presenting, recursively, an interpretation of death and
immortality, followed by a castrative text, followed, in turn, by another
discussion of death and immortality. Freud describes another story by
Hoffmann, "The Devil's Elixir," focusing here upon his use of the
theme of the double. His argument moves from the denial of death, to
the double as a portrayal of the immortality of the soul, to the double as
a defense against castration, to ancient Egyptian practices of creating
doubles to promote immortality, and finally to the double as herald of
death.

The double "was originally an insurance against the destruction of
the ego, an 'energetic denial of the power of death' . . . and probably the
'immortal' soul was the first 'double' of the body" (17: 235). Eventually,
he states, "from having been an assurance of immortality, [the double]

becomes the uncanny harbinger of death" (17: 235). Thus, the double evolves from a "protection against death to death's emissary" (Lydenberg 1997: 1081). In these passages, Freud virtually collapses the theory of castration into the theory of the death instinct. Although he elsewhere attempted to maintain the primacy of castration anxiety over death anxiety, here, the two are inseparable. These texts even hint that death takes primacy over castration. But Freud stops himself before making that move. Committed as he is to the Oedipal masterplot and the castration complex, he cannot fully pursue the implications of his own insights suggesting the primacy of the death drive over the castration complex.[11]

Three vivid images conclude the "collection of examples" in "The Uncanny": a castration image, an image of being buried alive, and an image of the mother's genitals. The dramatic castration image illustrates the master thesis Freud propounds in this text: "Dismembered limbs, a severed head, a hand cut off at the wrist . . . feet which dance by themselves . . . all these have something peculiarly uncanny about them." This kind of uncanniness, he argues, "springs from its proximity to the castration complex" (*SE* 17: 244). Freud's penultimate example, fear of living burial, is tentatively offered and subsequently retracted in a move which itself seems to compulsively repeat a pattern we have previously observed. Freud stated, "to many people the idea of being buried alive while appearing to be dead is the most uncanny thing of all. And yet psycho-analysis has taught us that this terrifying phantasy is only a transformation of another phantasy which had originally nothing terrifying about it at all but was filled with a certain lustful pleasure — the phantasy, I mean, of intra-uterine existence (*Leben im Mutterlieb*)." (*CP* 4: 397).[12] The terror of death through premature burial is thus diminished or transformed into pleasure by locating its source in the fantasy of returning to the womb. What seems uncanny is actually canny, comforting, pleasant, or cozy (*SE* 17: 222 n. 2). Freud's proffered and retracted image simultaneously illustrates and enacts the repetition compulsion. As in "A Religious Experience," "The Theme of the Three Caskets," "Medusa's Head," and the dream of the beaked birds, the fear of death is transformed into maternal/erotic love, death is transformed into sex, tomb transformed into womb. In what might be called a Freudian "*Heimlich* maneuver," the uncanniness of death through burial is displaced onto the canniness of the mother's genitals, which in this context signify pleasure, rather than death and burial.

This leads Freud directly to his final example of the uncanny. Introducing this image as "a beautiful confirmation of our theory of the uncanny" (by "our theory" he means here the theory of the source of the uncanny in the return of the repressed), he notes that, the previous example notwithstanding, male patients frequently report that "they feel there is something uncanny about the female genital organs." He explains: "This *unheimlich* place however is the entrance to the former *Heim* of all human beings, to the place where each one of us lived once upon a time and in the beginning ... we may interpret the place as being mother's genitals or her body. In this case too the *unheimlich* is what was once *heimisch*, homelike, familiar, the prefix 'un' (*un*) is the token of repression" (*SE* 17: 245, parentheses in original).

These images inscribe a powerful circularity: Freud links the uncanny with both birth and death. Human beginnings are linked with endings. Freud's own later autobiographical remark recapitulates this cycle: "The triumph of my life lies in my having, after a long and roundabout journey, found my way back to my earliest path" (*SE* 20: 253). Like the figure of the mother who gives birth and enfolds in death in "The Theme of the Three Caskets," these images return us to our place of origin, but leave us with an uncanny sense of alienation. The terror of premature burial is exposed as a pleasurable fantasy of returning to the mother's genitals, but the mother's genitals are in turn exposed as terrifying and uncanny. The final set of images — castration, premature burial, and maternal genitals — recapitulates the tension in the overall movement of the essay: an Oedipal/castrative master thesis is interrupted by a counterthesis suggesting that death and the mother are the primary factors invoking the uncanny.[13]

Freud linked the uncanny to religion very directly in the linguistic portion of his essay, quoting several biblical passages and theological texts. He cites Psalms 27: "In the secret of his tabernacle he shall hide me *heimlich*" (*SE* 17: 225), and he quotes Schelling, "To veil the divine, to surround it with a certain *Unheimlichkeit*" (*SE* 17: 224). While hiding in the house of God and veiling the divine are certainly *(un)heimlich,* it is the idea of the afterlife which is most closely related to our theme. The *unheimlich Heim,* the uncanny home, appears in another text of Freud's, a text which brings us directly into contact with the theme of religion and the afterlife: *The Future of an Illusion.*

In this famous book, Freud criticizes three central doctrines of Western religious thought: the idea of God, the idea of a moral universe, and the idea of a blissful afterlife. He argues that these "doctrines" are illusions or wishes: "It would be very nice if there were a God who created the world and was a benevolent Providence, and if there were a moral order in the universe, and an afterlife, but it is a very striking fact that all this is exactly as we are bound to wish it to be" (*SE* 21: 33). Such beliefs are direct and transparent expressions of human desires, "fulfillments of the oldest, strongest and most urgent wishes of mankind" (30).

Let us attend carefully to the words Freud uses to describe the psychological effect of religious notions of the presence of God and the reality of the afterlife. He describes "the painful riddle of death" and the uncertainties of life. One might suppose, he notes, that this "condition of things would result in a permanent state of anxious expectation." However, religion assuages these anxieties, offering promises of safety, predictability, and familiarity: "If death itself is not something spontaneous but the violent act of an evil will, if everywhere in nature there are beings around us of a kind that we know in our society, then we can breathe freely, can feel at home in the uncanny *[fühlt sich heimisch im Unheimlichen],* and can deal by psychical means with our senseless anxiety" (*SE* 21: 16–17; *GS* 11: 424). By negating death and affirming God, religion allows us to feel *"at home in the uncanny."* The words are not far from those he used in "The Uncanny" in describing the mother's genitals: the *unheimlich Heim,* the uncanny home, resonates richly with the "home in the uncanny."

In *The Future of an Illusion,* religious beliefs offer a home in the uncanny, a *Heim* in the *unheimlich,* a sense of familiarity in the unfamiliar. In "The Uncanny," the mother's body or the female genitals offer an image of an uncanny home, a sense of discomfort in the familiar. The *unheimlich,* uncanny, unfamiliar, maternal body is what was once *heimisch* or *heimlich,* familiar or "homey," while the *heimlich* (familiar) religious universe assuages the *unheimlich* disorientation of existential anxiety. Heaven and the mother's genitals are uncannily linked. The first makes us feel at home in the *Unheimlichkeit;* the latter makes us feel *unheimlich* at home. Religion offers at-homeness in the uncanny; the female genitals offer uncanniness at home. Pivotal in the *unheimlich Heimlichkeit* of each is "the riddle of death": religion's reconstruction of death into an illusion of a desirable afterlife is what makes it so *heimlich,* while the proximity of the maternal body to the symbolism of death is what makes it so *unheimlich.* Freud's texts delineate religion's reconstruction of the *unheimlich* facticity of life and death into the *heimlich* familiarity of God's universe. Freud's terminology exposes the presence of the maternal body in ideas about death and the afterlife.[14]

THE RENUNCIATION OF GOD
AND THE AFTERLIFE

Freud's texts on religion explicitly urge a renunciation of the belief in God the father. In his Oedipal paradigm, the atheist position on the question of God enacts a heroic, post-Oedipal stance whereby one overcomes the regressive tendency toward filial submission motivated by castration anxiety. Atheism thus constitutes a kind of courageous act of parricide. As Freud suggested in "Dostoevsky and Parricide," the slaying of the divine father through the abandonment of the belief in God is to be seen as a way of expressing an Oedipal or post-Oedipal victory over a judging and threatening father (*SE* 21: 177–94).

Within the context of the counterthesis, however, God's absence or God's negation appears closely linked to maternity, mortality, and immortality: the absence of God emerges as a central element within the non-Oedipal counterthesis. We noted earlier, for example, that Freud's parapraxes regarding God, nature, and the afterlife raised the possibility that the contemporary critique of God may be heavily overdetermined and overlaid with maternal connections. An exclusively Oedipal hermeneutic fails to inquire into the maternal pedagogies that may underlie atheism and disbelief. Similarly, the attachment to or abandonment of the belief in immortality and the afterlife involves non-Oedipal dynamics.[15]

Freud strongly urged the renunciation of the idea of the afterlife. Not only does the belief in the afterlife too readily fulfill our wishes, he argued, it also has harmful social effects. By promising a blissful future life for individuals, it prevents us from striving for universal justice in this life. In the utopian pages at the end of *The Future of an Illusion,* he sketches a glorious future for those who abandon the mythology of a heavenly afterlife: "By withdrawing their expectations from the other world and concentrating all their liberated energies into their life on earth, they will probably succeed in achieving a state of things in which life will become tolerable for everyone and civilization no longer oppressive to anyone. Then, with one of our fellow unbelievers, they will be able to say without regret, 'we leave heaven to the angels and the sparrows'" (*SE* 21: 50).

If our interpretation of Freud's incompletely developed counterthesis is correct, however, the abandonment of the belief in the afterlife is not as simple as it sounds, primarily because it is so intricately intertwined, to use Freud's terminology, "at the deeper layers" with notions of maternity and mortality (Jones 1957: 162). Freud saw his humanist and secularist negation of religion as an Oedipal or post-Oedipal challenge, but the counterthesis within his own work shows that his critique of the religious notion of the afterlife — and indeed, his atheist challenge to belief in God as well — cannot be fully understood within an Oedipal framework of parricidal and incestuous fantasies.

The Future of an Illusion, the text that most clearly negates God and the religious belief in the afterlife, suggests through its language that the "home in the uncanny" represented by religious ideas about a heavenly afterlife is a kind of mirrored reversal of the "uncanny home" represented by the mother's genitals. Freud's explicit recommendation is a renunciation of that desire for a heavenly home in the uncanny. His counterthesis, however, hints at the more complex entanglement of the notion of the afterlife with the fantasy of the uncanny home "where each one of us lived . . . in the beginning" (*SE* 17: 245).

These themes of immortality and the afterlife continue to be problematic today in the West, even as the discourse of immortality and the afterlife disappears from liberal religious rhetoric (Walter 1996) and reemerges in the literalized heavens of fundamentalist Protestant discourse, the angelology of popular culture, and the New Age discourses of reincarnation and past lives. Because the symbolic structures of earlier eras associated the body of the mother with death and the afterlife and supported these ideas upon a foundation of deep misogyny, contemporary variations of belief in immortality are likely to continue to serve as carriers for such fears and fantasies.

If Freud initiates but resists an inquiry into the interrelatedness of mortality, immortality, and maternity, he is not alone. Although the contemporary movement that focuses on the problems of death and dying seems to expose an eagerness for discussions of death (Bregman 1999), we more commonly evade talk about death — particularly when death is associated in any way with the mother. These are the topics of the unspeakable. Cultural and religious discourse idealizes motherhood and avoids open acknowledgment of matriphobic or matricidal fantasies. Similarly, contemporary secular discourse, uncomfortable with the traditional religious imagery of heaven, hell, and eternal life — and even with ideas about God — tends to evade serious consideration of fantasies of God, afterlife, and immortality. We have thus become increasingly hesitant to expose conscious or unconscious desires for God, immortality, and the afterlife which, if my reading of Freud's undeveloped counterthesis is correct, are intertwined with the matriphilic, matricidal, matriphobic, and misogynist fantasies of the unspeakable. These fantasies and desires require closer analysis. We can benefit from an attempt to disentangle our fears of death and our desires for immortality from our fears of mothers and fantasies of matricide.

CHAPTER 3

Jewishness
and the (Un)Canny
"Death and Us Jews"

Chapter 2 traced a "counterthesis" in Freud's writings in three kinds of images, each associated with death, immortality, and the afterlife: images of dead mothers, images of mothers as instructors in death, and images of uncanny maternal bodies. Showing that Freud used similar terminology to describe the heavenly afterlife (a "home in the uncanny") and the genitals of the mother ("an uncanny home"), I suggested that Freud's counterthesis hinted at a theory of unconscious associations of maternity, mortality, and immortality. This chapter will pursue this excavation of Freud's notion of the uncanny at another set of sites: the counterthesis appears vividly in Freud's descriptions of his own Jewish identity, particularly when he is speaking privately to fellow Jews. In these remarks, he initiates a fragmentary analysis of the attractions and dangers of Jewish assimilationism.

An examination of recent literature on Freud's Jewish identity will introduce a discussion of Judaism, gender, and psychoanalysis. Then, connections will be drawn between Freud's Jewish identity and the notion of the "uncanny Jew," showing that Freud attempted in "The Uncanny" to displace and reenvision this widespread trope. Finally, the complexities of Freud's own sense of the *(Un)Heimlichkeit* of Jewish identity will be exposed through a discussion of two essays written for the Viennese Jewish fellowship, the B'nai B'rith, one of which exists in both its original version and in a more public version stripped of its uniquely Jewish elements.

FREUD'S JEWISH IDENTITY

Freud's own pronouncements regarding his Jewish identity are conflicted. Early letters reveal attempts to define himself as an educated, assimilated, Western European Jew, rather than an *Ostjude,* a Jew of Eastern Europe associated in the dominant ideologies with religious orthodoxy and shtetl origins. During the formative years of the psychoanalytic movement, concerned lest psychoanalysis be dismissed as "a Jewish science" or a "Jewish national affair" (Abraham and Freud 1965: 34), he claimed an objective, impersonal, scientific provenance for his creation. Later, although he continued to proclaim himself "estranged" from all religions, he identified himself as a Jew "in his essential nature" (*SE* 13: xv). And he famously described himself as a "godless" and "infidel Jew" (*SE* 21: 170), rhetorically asking his colleague, the Protestant pastor and psychoanalyst Oskar Pfister, why the world had to wait for a "godless Jew" to discover psychoanalysis (Jones 1955: 507, Meng and Freud 1963: 63).

Freud's own diverse comments, both positive and negative, regarding his Jewish identity have become pieces of a shifting sense of Freud in the collective memory of our culture. In this fluid remembrance or reconstruction, Freud has played a range of roles: he has been portrayed as a nonreligious secular scientist without a significant Jewish identity, a faithful, although conflicted Jew, and a secular Jew struggling with assimilationist desires and anti-Semitic forces.

These reconstructions reveal as much about variations in cultural concerns as they do about Freud himself (Miller 1981). Until midcentury, a Gentile or secularized intellectual culture, idealizing science and desiring to protect Freud from his anti-Semitic detractors, defended Freud as a great theorist whose Jewishness was merely incidental

(Wittels 1924, Jones 1953, 1955, 1957, and, more recently, Gay 1987). Later scholars, less concerned about the dangers of anti-Semitism, some of whom were interested in reclaiming and legitimating Freud's Jewishness, took the opposite view, arguing that Freud was essentially Jewish and that his Jewish origins were central in the development of psychoanalysis (Bakan 1958). A third group of predominantly secular or postreligious theorists began to ask complex questions about Freud's Jewish identity and his cultural/historical context, arguing that psychoanalysis emerged as a sort of compromise between the conflicting demands of secular and scientific modernity and Jewish traditionalism (Miller 1981: 357, Homans 1989, Rieff 1966, Ricoeur 1970).

In the contemporary period, this concern with the effect of modernity and traditionalism on Freud's work has deepened as a group of scholars in Jewish studies concerned with an exploration of the effects of anti-Semitism have begun to uncover in the background of psychoanalysis the forces of anti-Jewish ideologies (Geller 1997, Gilman 1993), Jewish traditionalism (Handelman 1982, Klein 1985, Rice 1990, Yerushalmi 1991, Roith 1987), assimilationism (Schorske 1973, McGrath 1986, Le Rider 1993), and the broader forces of secularization (Homans 1989, 1995 [1979]). In some of this literature, the reconstruction of Freud's Jewishness has undergone yet another turn in which the construction of gender and sexuality within the context of anti-Semitism is interrogated as a component of the Jewish origins of psychoanalysis. Many of the scholars engaged in this project have been influenced by feminist theory, cultural studies, and queer theory (Geller 1992a, 1992b, 1993, 1997, 1999, Gilman 1993, Jacobs 1997, Boyarin 1994, 1997, Le Rider 1993, Eilberg-Schwartz 1994). A dominant view among many of the scholars of this last group is that Freud's concern — conscious or unconscious — was to "masculinize" Jewishness in an attempt to negate a racist ideology widespread in nineteenth-century central Europe within which male Jews were seen as degenerate, inferior, and feminine or effeminate.

My interpretation of the gendering of Judaism and anti-Semitism in

Freud's life and theory differs in some important ways from the generally accepted view in this body of literature. I agree with these scholars
that much of Freud's work enacted a response to the anti-Semitic gendering of the male Jew as feminine. I find in Freud's writings, however,
not only an attempt to masculinize Judaism,[1] but also an attempt (usually incomplete or interrupted, but an attempt nevertheless) to analyze
and interpret ways in which Jewishness is ideologically and unconsciously gendered as feminine both for the Jew and the anti-Semite.
Freud struggled to theorize associations of Jewishness with the uncanny, the mother, death, and immortality within the unconscious psyche.[2] A brief survey of the literature on psychoanalysis, Judaism, and
gender will establish a foundation for an analysis of the emergence of
these elements of the counterthesis in Freud's texts on his Jewish identity in this chapter and an analysis of the emergence of the counterthesis in his writings on anti-Semitism in the next.

In a series of significant publications, Sander Gilman has argued that
Freud's theories represent unconscious reactions to or at times conscious
reversals of the racist and misogynist rhetoric of anti-Semitism. In
Gilman's view, Freud's work on gender enacts a massive and misogynist defense against anti-Semitic ideologies: Freud developed a theory
of gender within which the racial rhetoric of Jewish inferiority was displaced onto a theory of female inferiority. Gilman exposes Freud's reaction to the pejorative anti-Semitic rhetoric of medical texts and popular
literature at the turn of the century. He states, "in Freud's scientific
writing this set of images was transferred exclusively to the image of
women." He concludes that "the rhetoric of race was excised from
Freud's scientific writing and appeared only in his construction of gender" (1993: 37). Freud's theories, in his view, are thus a defense against
and a displacement of the racism of his time. In this context, Gilman
argues, Freud insistently encoded Judaism as male, conceptualizing science as a masculine space where male Jewish scientists could escape the
feminizing definitions of their culture. In a set of related publications,
Jay Geller has exposed the widespread association of male Jews with

women in the anti-Semitic ideologies of Freud's time, arguing that Freud's rejection of this feminization of Jewishness underlies his texts on religion and culture.

Many of Gilman's and Geller's conclusions confirm and contextualize those of Judith van Herik, who showed in *Freud on Faith and Femininity* that Freud's description of Judaism in *Moses and Monotheism* and of science in *The Future of an Illusion* match precisely his description of Oedipal masculinity as a capacity for moral renunciation and intellectual courage. Gilman's work establishes the cultural and historical context within which we can better understand the vision of science as a form of "ideal" masculinity uncovered by Van Herik in Freud's cultural texts. Van Herik also showed that Freud's description of Christian religious belief in *The Future of an Illusion* reiterates his description of Oedipal femininity as a wish-fulfilling relation of dependence upon a father. Geller's research provides an important context within which to understand Van Herik's thesis regarding Freud's feminization of Christian religious belief. As a Jewish male in a misogynist and anti-Semitic world which feminized Jewish males, Freud turned the tables by subtly underscoring the psychological femininity of Christian belief and the psychological masculinity of renunciatory Jewish morality and intellect.

Daniel Boyarin develops these arguments further. He suggests that Freud's Jewishness and the origins of psychoanalytic theory cannot be fully understood without attention to two important issues. The first is the acceptance and honoring of an alternate model of masculinity within Judaism prior to the 1890s, specifically, the idealization of the gentle, scholarly male, rather than the muscular, stoic male who was idealized in the dominant cultural discourses. The second is the dramatic cultural shift in the understanding of heterosexuality and homosexuality in fin de siècle Europe, which led to the renunciation of this alternate pattern of masculinity. Boyarin states, "there is something correct — although seriously misguided — in the persistent European representation of the Jewish man as a sort of woman. More than just an antisemitic stereotype, the Jewish ideal male as countertype to 'manliness' is an assertive historical product of Jewish culture" (1997: 3–4). Yet Boyarin agrees with Gilman and Geller that the central tenets of psychoanalysis developed during and after the 1890s represent in some sense an attempt to masculinize the Jewish male through a rhetoric that approximated that of the muscular masculinity of the dominant culture. In addition, he agrees with these theorists that Freud attempted with his theories to negate any possible associations of Jewish masculinities with homosexuality. He traces a complex recoding of race and gender in Freud's thought: "feminization and homosexuality were 'Jewish diseases' that Freud was anxious to overcome, and once overcome, they could safely be pathologized" (Boyarin 1997: 219).[3]

A dominant view among these scholars is that Freud's writings attempt a "hypermasculinization" (Geller 1993: 62) of Jewishness in the context of an anti-Semitic representation of the Jewish male as feminine and effeminate and the context of a secularist representation of science as masculine. This perspective is quite accurate, although this is not the whole story. Freud did, indeed, portray Judaism in ways he and his culture coded as masculine. The overarching framework of *Moses and Monotheism* provides striking evidence of this masculinizing pattern. There he described Jewish monotheism as "an advance in intellect" (*SE* 23: 128–29) and an advance in ethics (68), precisely the "advances" *(Fortschritten)* he associated with males and masculinity in this and other texts. This inscription of ethical and intellectual advances as masculine is hinted at in a text quoted earlier, *The Ego and the Id:* "religion, morality, and a social sense — the chief elements in the higher side of man — were . . . acquired phylogenetically out of the father-complex. . . . The male sex seems to have taken the lead in all these moral acquisitions" (*SE* 19: 37).

Similarly, Freud argued in *Moses and Monotheism* that Jewish aniconicity, the objection to the visual portrayal of God, honors intellectual abstraction over sensory perception in a "triumph of intellectuality over sensuality" paralleling the victory of fatherhood or patriarchy

(Vaterschaft) over matriarchy and of monotheism over the cults of mother goddesses (*SE* 23: 113–14, 46). Freud thus described Judaism as a form of religion intellectually and morally more advanced than either polytheism or Christianity in terms closely matching his descriptions of Oedipal masculinity. Van Herik describes Freud's assumptions: "followers of the Mosaic tradition . . . follow the masculine path of Oedipal renunciation of instinct under the law of the father; they achieve its economic correlates: advance in intellectuality, culture, and morality" (1982: 178). Boyarin, as well, notes that Freud's point in *Moses and Monotheism* "was to argue that Hebrew monotheism was a religion of manliness, self defense, and self control" (1997: 249). In other words, Freud did indeed "masculinize" Judaism.

The masculinization of Judaism in *Moses and Monotheism* and other works expresses Freud's Oedipal master thesis and erects a barrier against anti-Semitic accusations of Jewish effeminacy. Yet although many of Freud's texts emphasize the masculinity of Jewishness, another narrative also lies between the lines. This other narrative is about Jewishness, mothers, and femininity, rather than Jewishness, fathers, and masculinity. This is not only a story of internalizations of racist ideologies of effeminate Jews, although, as Jacobs, Gilman, and others show, that pattern is certainly in evidence. Nor are the mothers of this other story the erotic mothers of the Oedipal son's incestuous fantasies. Rather, these mothers — consistently Jewish mothers — are associated with death, loss, immortality, and the uncanny. This story leads us not only to another site at which Freud's counterthesis spilled over into his texts, but also to an incompletely developed analysis of the duality of *Heimlichkeit* and *Unheimlichkeit,* the simultaneous "canniness" and uncanniness of Jewishness to the Jew. It leads, in other words, to an analysis of the inevitable ambivalence of central European fin de siècle Jews about their own Jewishness.[4]

In this analysis, Freud struggled to ask about the unconscious meanings of Jewish identity for Jews. As we shall see in the next chapter, he also struggled to ask about the unconscious meanings of Jewishness for anti-Semites. He was, in a sense, articulating through his theory the crises of sexual identity and Jewish identity that Le Rider identifies as the central crisis of Viennese fin de siècle modernity, calling it the "triangle of masculine, feminine, and Jew" (1993: 171).

Freud was engaged not only in a defensive denial of femininity and homosexuality in the male Jew, he was also engaged in an analysis of the ways in which anti-Semitism, homophobia, and misogyny are intimately interconnected in the unconscious (cf. Boyarin 1997: 17).

THE JEW AND THE UNCANNY

In the preceding chapter, we saw that Freud linked the maternal body, death, and the afterlife with the uncanny in his famous essay "The Uncanny" ("Das Unheimliche"). In that essay, he did *not* explicitly link the uncanny with Jews, Judaism, or Jewishness. The image of the uncanny Jew, however, undergirds that essay as a set of psychological and cultural associations.

Widespread in nineteenth-century European culture was a notion of the Jewish people as uncanny. Jews were described as occupying a position on the border between life and death; they were envisioned as lacking a national home *(Heimlos);* they were said to be "unwelcome guests and aliens wandering into and within other people's homes, disrupting and haunting them" (Shapiro 1997: 65). Foundational to this image was the popular notion that Christianity emerged from and transcended Judaism, making Judaism unnecessary and archaic. Surveying this ideology in "The Uncanny Jew: A Brief History of an Image," Susan Shapiro cites a number of Central European documents from the late nineteenth and early twentieth centuries in which, for example, Ahasuerus, the "eternal Jew" or "wandering Jew," is described as an uncanny living corpse, a "dead man who has not died" (Shapiro 1997: 63).

In Shapiro's view, Freud's essay "The Uncanny" is constructed directly upon this trope. She suggests that Freud shifts the rhetoric of the uncanny from uncanny Jew to uncanny maternal body by locating the uncanny in the fantasy of the return to the mother's genitals: "The uncanny is thereby displaced from the Jewish male and grafted onto the body of woman, especially as mother. The primary anxiety which produces this sense of *'Unheimlichkeit'* is located in this way not in racial terms, but explicitly in sexual difference" (1997: 71). Unlike Gilman, however, who finds such displacements essentially defensive, Shapiro finds it analytic and interpretive. She argues that it is precisely the "trope of the uncanny Jew that Freud is both displacing and attempting to re-envision" (Shapiro 1997: 70).

Shapiro's insight that Freud is both displacing and attempting to re-envision the trope of the uncanny Jew is exactly on the mark. Like Shapiro, I find in Freud's work an attempt to theorize and re-envision the psychological and cultural meanings of the uncanny Jew and the uncanny mother, the living/dead Jew, and the deadly yet life-giving mother. We shall encounter the themes of wandering, homelessness, and "living death" again and again in Freud's texts as he displaces and re-envisions the notion of the uncanny Jew.

One site of this displacing and re-envisioning is an anecdote Freud recounts in "The Uncanny" in which he brings together the theme of wandering and the experience of the uncanny. Without referring explicitly to his Jewish identity, he portrays himself as a wanderer far from home who experiences a sense of the uncanny when he loses his way in a labyrinth of female sexuality which leads to death. The trope of the uncanny Jew lies just below the surface of this text. Let us look closely at this passage.

Freud introduces the passage on his wanderings by framing it as an example of the emergence of a sense of the uncanny through repetition. He states:

> As I was walking, one hot summer afternoon, through the deserted
> streets of a provincial town in Italy which was unknown to me,
> I found myself in a quarter of whose character I could not long
> remain in doubt. Nothing but painted women were to be seen at
> the windows of the small houses, and I hastened to leave the nar-

row street at the next turning. But after having wandered about for a time without inquiring my way, I suddenly found myself back in the same street where my presence was now beginning to excite attention. I hurried away once more, only to arrive by another detour at the same place yet a third time. Now, however, a feeling overcame me which I can only describe as uncanny, and I was glad enough to find myself back at the piazza I had left a short while before, without any further voyages of discovery. (*SE* 17: 237)

Freud's narrative paints a vivid picture: the reader visualizes the Viennese Jew hurrying through hot Italian streets unable to escape the gaze of the "painted women" and unable to cease his "wanderings." He distances his wanderings from the path of Ahasuerus, the wandering Jew, by calling them "voyages of discovery" (*Entdeckungsreisen, GS* 10: 389), implying a heroic, goal-directed quest. Freud's experience of uncanniness in this circumstance emerges, however, not only because he is lost or entrapped in a maze of sexuality and under the gaze of desiring women, but also because he is here traversing the path of the uncanny/wandering Jew, displacing and attempting to re-envision the trope. He found the experience so uncanny precisely because he was confronting the stereotype of the uncanny Jew head-on.

It is particularly significant that his very next example of the uncanny in the essay involves the expectation of death and the theme of survival. In a sense, he reiterates the theme of the dead/undead Olympia, whom we discussed in the previous chapter, alongside the theme of the living corpse of the uncanny Jew described by Shapiro. He states:

We naturally attach no importance to the event when we hand in an overcoat and get a cloakroom ticket with the number, let us say, 62; or when we find that our cabin on a ship bears that number. But the impression is altered if two such events happen . . . close together. If we come across the number 62 several times in a single day . . . we feel this to be uncanny. And unless a man is utterly hardened and proof against the lure of superstition, he will be tempted to ascribe a secret meaning to this obstinate recurrence of a number; he will take it, perhaps as an indication of the span of life allotted to him. (*SE* 17: 237–38)[5]

The number sixty-two was indeed an uncanny one for Freud. For many years he had superstitiously expected to die at age sixty-two. As he told Carl Jung in a letter of 1909, fate had in fact put into his path numerous examples of the number sixty-two, in telephone numbers, coat checks, and theater tickets (McGuire 1974: 219). Writing this essay in 1919, Freud had just passed the uncanny age of his expected demise — and, to draw a larger connection to death and survival — he, his family, and his movement had survived the "Great War." Now, at age sixty-three, he could look back on his superstitious expectation of death with some detachment and analytic acumen. The wandering Jew, fated to die at age sixty-two, had survived. Cixous asks, "Isn't the one who has lived a year beyond the age foreseen for his own disappearance in some way, a ghost?" (1976: 541). He is not only a ghost, however. In this text, he is also an uncanny Jew: dead and undead (age sixty-three), homeless (walking through deserted streets of a town "unknown to me") and wandering (lost). All the elements Shapiro links with the uncanny Jew lie within the text. The key components of the counterthesis, sexuality, death, and immortality, are present, as well.

Consciously or unconsciously Freud identified with the wandering Jew in this passage on painted women, death, and the uncanny. This identification is reiterated by a letter, mentioned in chapter 1, that he wrote to one of his sons twenty years after the publication of this text. In this letter, written just prior to his departure for England and freedom from a Vienna under Nazi occupation, Freud explicitly identified with Ahasuerus. Comparing England to ancient Egypt, he stated, "I sometimes compare myself with the old Jacob who, when a very old man, was taken by his children to Egypt. . . . Let us hope that it won't also be followed by an exodus from Egypt. It is high time that Ahasuerus came to rest somewhere" (E. Freud 1992: 298). The identification with the wandering Jew is acknowledged explicitly in the document of 1938. It is close to the surface of the text in the wandering "voyages of discovery" of the 1919 essay, "The Uncanny," as well.

TWO PRESENTATIONS TO THE B'NAI B'RITH

The notion of the *Heimlichkeit* and/or *Unheimlichkeit* of Jewishness is evident in other texts, too. Freud's own words expose the mirror image of the uncanny Jew, the "canny" Jew, in an essay presented to the B'nai B'rith. In 1926, in honor of his seventieth birthday, the B'nai B'rith lodge in Vienna invited Freud to present a talk. He had spoken to this community of Jewish men a number of times, particularly during the crucial early years of the development of psychoanalysis, when he had found a supportive group of friends and colleagues in the group (Klein 1985).[6] In his seventieth-birthday address, which, because of ill health, he did not deliver in person, he looked back upon his longtime association with the B'nai B'rith, describing his initial motives for joining the group and emphasizing his early sense of comfort in the community. He wrote, "That you were Jews could only be agreeable to me." What had made "the attraction of Jewry and Jews irresistible," he continued, involved (in Strachey's translation in the *Standard Edition*) "many obscure emotional forces which were the more powerful the less they could be expressed in words, as well as a clear consciousness of inner identity, the safe privacy of a common mental construction" (*SE* 20: 273–74). The term translated in the *Standard Edition* as "safe privacy" is Freud's *Heimlichkeit.* Freud's phrase is "die Heimlichkeit der gleichen seelischen Konstruktion" (*GS* 20: 50). To bring Freud's terminology to the surface, a better translation of the phrase might be "the canniness [or familiarity] of a common psychic structure."[7]

In the comfortable milieu of the B'nai B'rith, surrounded by a fraternity of fellow Jews, Freud affirmed a canny commonality or familiarity of psyche, intellect, or soul: Jewish identity is *heimlich,* it is like being "at home." But to Freud, Jewishness is not only *heimlich,* but also *unheimlich.* Reading his remarks to the B'nai B'rith alongside his essay "The Uncanny," we recall from the previous chapter that *heimlich* "is a word the meaning of which develops toward an ambivalence until it coincides with its opposite, *unheimlich.*" The uncanny, as we have seen, is associated with fears of being castrated and being buried alive, death, the mother, and immortality (*SE* 17: 244–45). Freud's experience of Jewishness is part of that extended complex.

Support for this can be found not only in Shapiro's analysis of the trope of the uncanny Jew, but also in the work of David Bakan. In an essay on *Heimlichkeit* which concludes *Sigmund Freud and the Jewish Mystical Tradition,* Bakan draws conclusions which intersect with my own. Introducing a theme we have encountered earlier, Bakan notes, "If *Heim* is associated with being Jewish and *Unheim* with death, and these two are, as Freud tells us, to be identified, then Freud's Jewish feeling is related to his sense of impending death" (1958: 314–15).[8] Bakan also draws connections between the *Heimlichkeit* of Judaism and the *Unheimlichkeit* of the body of the mother in Freud's texts. Citing the concluding passages of "The Uncanny" in which, as we have seen, Freud associates the uncanny with the mother's genitals and calls the mother's genitals our "first home," Bakan argues:

> That Freud should refer to the female genitals as home (*Heim*) is
> not at all strange. For the Jews, who in the Diaspora had no land,
> who always had a sense of temporariness in connection with their
> dwelling places, the mother, the wife, is the home. With his sense of
> impending death, Freud is then returning home. As is suggested by
> his speech to the B'nai B'rith, he is returning to membership in the
> body of Israel. (1958: 316)

Although Bakan displaces Freud's emphasis from the genitals to the body and from a physical mother's body to a spiritual body of Israel, his point is nevertheless significant. Jewish identity, the uncanny, and the mother's body are inseparable in Freud's texts.[9] Bakan observes as well the presence of the theme of immortality in association with the uncanny: "Freud's sense of *Heimlichkeit* is a return to the classical legends of a life after death which, in Judaism, is associated with the mystical cultural atmosphere" (1958: 315).

For Bakan, this uncanny association of Judaism, circumcision, death, mother, and immortality provides evidence to support his thesis that Freud was heavily influenced by Jewish mystical traditions in his development of psychoanalytic ideas.[10] While Bakan's broad interest in Jewish influences on psychoanalysis has served to spark a large body of literature on Judaism and psychoanalysis, the specific thesis he developed regarding the direct influence of the Jewish mystical tradition on psychoanalysis remains controversial. Some scholars support Bakan's thesis (Roith 1987, Merkur 1997), but most maintain that Freud's contact with Jewish mystical ideas was indirect or that the psychoanalytic technique of interpretation that Bakan found so similar to Kabbalistic interpretation is not specific to Kabbalah, but rather was a component of the rabbinical tradition shared broadly by European Jews (Handleman 1982, Frieden 1990). Many of Bakan's core observations, however, can be supported. We need not postulate specific knowledge, conscious or unconscious, of the Jewish mystical traditions underlying Freud's ideas in order to reclaim Bakan's understanding of the uncanniness of Judaism and its association with the body of the mother, with death, and with immortality.[11] This psychological and cultural complex of ideas is evident in the trope of the uncanny, *unheimlich* Jew, as well as in Freud's remarks on the "intimacy," *Heimlichkeit,* of his connection with the members of the B'nai B'rith.

Bakan is particularly interested in the *Heimlichkeit,* the comfort, familiarity, and sense of home associated with the mother. My concern is both with this *Heimlichkeit* and the *Unheimlichkeit* associated with the mother, her deadly, dangerous qualities and her association with the absence of God. Bakan hypothesized a literal, historical contact with mystical ideas. I find instead a set of textual, cultural, psychological associations. But I agree with Bakan that for Freud, Judaism itself is associated with the uncanny, the mother, immortality, and death — and with

Shapiro who, as we have seen, finds within Freud's writings on the uncanny the shadowy image of the uncanny Jew. These connections have been obscured by the more visible coding of Judaism as masculine or "hypermasculine" within the terms of Freud's Oedipal thesis.

These associations are clearly suggested in the 1926 B'nai B'rith text. A dramatic example of another text by Freud associating Jewishness with the uncanny, the mother, death, and immortality can be found in a 1915 presentation to the B'nai B'rith, the same group to whom Freud directed his seventieth-birthday remarks. In 1915, Freud presented an address entitled "Death and Us." This text, published in its initial format ("Wir und der Tod," 1915), was later revised for publication under a different title. The revision appeared in the psychoanalytic periodical *Imago* in 1916 as the second half of "Thoughts for the Times on War and Death" (*SE* 14: 289–300). The 1915 publication was virtually forgotten, to be rediscovered only recently, discussed briefly by Dennis Klein in *The Jewish Origins of the Psychoanalytic Movement* (1985), and translated into English only in 1993 (Solms, in Freud 1993).

This 1915 text is quite remarkable. It is one of the few texts available in two distinct versions, one version presented to a lay audience of fellow Jews, the second published in a "scientific," psychoanalytic journal. While rough drafts and notes for some of Freud's major works have been compared to his published works (Grubrich-Simitis 1996), this is the only text existing in two versions written more or less simultaneously for two different audiences (Solms, in Freud 1993, 4–5). The two texts are significantly different: one emphasizes Jewishness, the other does not.

Although Klein dismisses the differences between the two texts, arguing that the focus on the Jews in the B'nai B'rith essay was simply "an elocutionary device to sustain the interest of his audience" (1985: 92), I find the differences striking. One text foregrounds the sense of *Heimlichkeit* that Freud felt among his Jewish colleagues and mentioned explicitly in the 1926 address. The other eliminates the discussion of *Heimlichkeit,* universalizing the argument. The earlier text reinscribes the association of the Jew, death, the mother, immortality, and the uncanny, while the later text excises these associations. Tensions between the private Freud and the public Freud, between Freud the Jew and Freud the scientist, emerge with clarity. The differences and gaps between the two texts provide a dramatic illustration of Freud's comment that "things Jewish" are things to be spoken of only "among ourselves."

In the later text, "all passages of exclusively Jewish interest are expunged" (Solms, in Freud 1993: 7). These expunged references include an uncanny set of associations. The opening lines of the lecture contain a vivid example of the association of Judaism with the idea of death. Freud introduces his theme, the attitude of the unconscious toward death, by noting that he nearly selected as a title for the lecture, "Death and Us Jews": "instead of 'Death and Us,' it could have read: 'Death and Us Jews,' for it is precisely we Jews who reveal most frequently and in the most extreme ways the attitude towards death that I wish to deal with before you today" (Freud 1993: 11). This passage is simply eliminated from the version published in *Imago*. Mentioning the B'nai B'rith essay in a letter to his Jewish colleague Ferenczi (April 8, 1915), Freud called it "an audacious lecture" *(ein kecker Vortrag)* containing much "grim humor" *(Galgenhumor)* (Jones 1955: 415). Much of the audacity and the "grim" or "gallows" humor is missing from the more public text. The death jokes were, in a sense, inside jokes, Jewish jokes. Let us examine carefully this "audacious" text and its pale counterpart.

Both texts describe the unconscious denial of death and the disbelief in one's own mortality which, as we have seen, Freud would also describe in 1920 in *Beyond the Pleasure Principle*. He argues that life is impoverished when we deny the presence of death in the midst of life, that life is diminished in substance and meaning with the elimination of death as an inevitability. He goes on to examine the fear of death which, paradoxically but inevitably, accompanies the denial of death: because of our denial of mortality, "we dare not contemplate ... attempts at artificial flight, voyages of discovery to distant countries, or experiments with explosive substances" ("Death and Us," 1993: 16; cf. *SE* 14: 291). In the B'nai B'rith text, but not in the *Imago* text, he provides a "characteristic Jewish anecdote" to illustrate his point. "Take what one of our very characteristic Jewish anecdotes expresses: the son falls off a ladder, remains lying there unconscious, and the mother runs to the Rabbi to seek help and advice. 'Tell me,' asks the Rabbi, 'how does a Jewish child come to be on a ladder in the first place?'" (1993: 16–17).

Freud often utilized Jewish anecdotes in his writings, drawing upon their "profound and often bitter worldly wisdom" (*SE* 4: 195). The profound and bitter wisdom of this anecdote is quite apparent. Although Freud felt no need to offer further analysis of its meaning, some of the threads can be untangled. Climbing ladders should be avoided, the anecdote suggests. Such actions represent forbidden "attempts at artificial flight" which fail to respect the unconscious (and, according to this text, particularly Jewish) fear of death. Such activities represent, as well, we can assume, a dangerously assimilated, goyish, or non-Jewish adventurousness.[12] The mother who allowed the ascent sanctioned just such a non-Jewish "voyage of discovery" leading to her child's unconsciousness, or to his death. Gravity brought the child down to earth; the Rabbi brought the mother down to earth, chiding her for challenging the unconscious law of fear of death and chiding her as well for letting her son behave in such a goyish manner. The anecdote condenses unconscious fears of death, unconscious fears of deadly mothers, and Jewish fears of assimilation.

Freud's own analysis of the unconscious attitude toward death and his use of this particular anecdote situate him as one who challenges "unconscious laws," one who climbs ladders, one who initiates "voyages of discovery to distant countries" — such as the distant terrain of the unconscious — and one who experiments with "explosive substances," or at least with explosive ideas. Freud's account of the anecdote ruefully acknowledges unconscious expectations of punishment from reality and opprobrium from rabbis for disobeying the unconscious mandate that mothers and sons must simultaneously deny and fear death. In addition, it hints at expectations of punishment for his adventurous, goyish actions, behaviors, and desires. Absent from the more public version of the paper, the "characteristically Jewish anecdote" clearly highlights, for a Jewish audience, an association of Jewish religious ideas, mothers, assimilation, and death. And it echoes Freud's memory of his own Jewish mother and her lesson in mortality discussed in the preceding chapter.

Both texts contain a reference to the "motto of the Hanseatic League," which is contrasted with the paralyzing unconscious fear of death: "It is necessary to sail the seas, it is not necessary to live" (1993: 16, *SE* 14: 291). The Hanseatic League, a commercial and military association (Hansa) of medieval northern German coastal cities, controlled travel on the Baltic and North Seas, defended members against aggressors, developed laws of commercial exchange, and constructed navigational charts and routes (Dollinger 1970). While the league and its motto are present in both texts, in the B'nai B'rith text, the motto serves as an introduction to and inversion of the message expressed in the "characteristic Jewish anecdote." Freud draws a comparison between "we," the Jews who are paralyzed by concern with family ties and the fear of the loss of loved ones, and "they," the Hanseatic League of intrepid Germanic navigators:

> We dare not contemplate a great many undertakings which are dangerous but in fact indispensable. . . . We are paralyzed by the thought of who is to take the son's place with his mother, the husband's with his wife, the father's with his children if a disaster should occur, and yet all these undertakings are essential. You know the motto of the Hanseatic League: *Navigare necesse est, vivere non necesse.* It is necessary to sail the seas, it is not necessary to live. In comparison, take what one of our very characteristic Jewish anecdotes expresses . . . (1993: 16; cf. *SE* 14: 291)

Freud's contrast between the "undertakings" of the Hanseatic League and the "undertakings" that we "dare not contemplate" is multilayered. To his 1915 Jewish audience, Freud's reference would have communicated a complex message about Germanic anti-Semitism: the league was not only a group of explorers, navigators, and merchants, it was also a group which denied residency to Jews in its cities and discouraged Jewish commercial interests. To a Germany constructed upon economic anti-Jewish sentiment, "Hansa is good commerce, Jews bad."[13]

Freud knew his Jewish audience was well familiar with the Hanseatic League: "*you know* the motto of the Hanseatic League," he said (16, emphasis mine). His audience would also have recognized his contrast between the familial ties linking the Jews and the territorial and state ties linking the Germanic Hansa. The trope of the uncanny *(unheimlich)* Jews, homeless *(heimlos),* nationless, or stateless, was, as noted above, widespread in European thought. Freud's reference also emphasized familial fear for the safety of the son and concern with the mother's possible loss of her son: "We are paralyzed by the thought of who is to take the son's place with his mother . . . if a disaster should occur" (16). The accompanying anecdote suggests that the disastrous loss of the son may be a result of an uncanny and deadly mother, part of whose dangerous uncanniness lies in her tendency to behave like the mothers of the Hanseatic League. The dangerous mother makes of her son a goyish explorer and assimilationist ladder climber, rather than a Jewish son who stays in his "place with his mother" (16). Self-reflexively, and in the presence of his fellow Jews, Freud takes the side of the Hanseatic adventurer, a dangerous, goyish path of the navigator who may never return to "his place with his mother." Freud's text thus evokes a complex set of resonances in which the dangerous, but attractive Jewish assimilation to Gentile culture becomes part of the danger associated with the uncanny mother.[14]

Freud's self-identification as a navigator and adventurer had been foreshadowed several years earlier in the famous letter to Fliess mentioned above in which he called himself a *"conquistador"* and "adventurer." In this passage, often quoted in isolation, Freud actually goes on to express anxiety regarding the possible failure of the conquistador's efforts:

> I am by temperament, nothing but a *conquistador* — an adventurer
> if you want it translated — with all the curiosity, daring and tenacity
> characteristic of a man of this sort. Such people are customarily
> esteemed only if they have been successful, have really discovered
> something. Otherwise they are dropped by the wayside and that is
> not altogether unjust. At the present time, however, luck has left
> me. I no longer discover anything worthwhile. (Masson 1985: 398)

Thus, we see a repetition of an important theme: in the 1900 letter and in the 1915 address, each time speaking to fellow Jews, Freud identifies himself with a navigator and *"conquistador,"* but also expresses concern about possible failure, a failure which, as we've seen, is associated with mothers and death.

But let us return to Freud's reference to familial concerns in the 1915 texts. The concerns are evident in both texts, although in the *Imago* essay the passage is stripped of its Jewish components in a universalization of the emphasis on family ties and fear of loss. The transformation provides a story about universal human relations of mothers and sons in which the fear of death becomes not a Jewish fear of death, but a universal, human, unconscious fear of death. In the *Imago* version, "we" refers no longer to "we Jews," but to "we humans."

It is relevant to note that the tension between "we Jews" and "we humans" evident in the two versions of this text was echoed in Freud's personal life at this time. His break with Jung, the Gentile who, he had hoped, would universalize psychoanalysis, saving it from dismissal as a "Jewish science," was recent and still very painful. Replacing Jung as confidante and collaborator was his fellow Jew, Karl Abraham. Freud and Abraham commented frequently in correspondence on their "religoracial, psychological bond," their sense of being united as "we Jews" (Homans 1989: 36). Freud stated, for example, in correspondence with Abraham, "May I say that it is consanguineous Jewish traits *[dass es verwandte, jüdische Züge sind]* that attract me to you? We understand each other" (Abraham and Freud 1965: 46).

Freud's two audiences for the 1915 text on the fear of death, then — the scientific audience of *Imago* and the Jewish audience of the B'nai B'rith lecture — were paralleled by two primary personal audiences for his ideas: Jung and Abraham. Freud's remarks on the adventurer who must sail the seas but need not live and on the son who climbs ladders and falls may emerge from his own sense of having adventured into an uncanny and dangerous Hanseatic League of sorts alongside Carl Jung. His retreat to his Jewish colleagues, especially Karl Abraham, in this time of crisis and transition, may lie behind his emphasis on the family ties, fears of separation, and fears of death which "paralyze us."

Besides the explicit emphasis on the fear of death in relation to the son's place with the mother, both essays also speculate on another element associated with the uncanny. This element is immortality. Freud initiated in this text an inquiry into the origins of the belief in immortality, spirits, and the afterlife. The pain felt at the death of someone deeply loved, Freud suggests, led "primeval man" to the denial that death is annihilation: "It was beside the body of someone he loved that he made up spirits . . . in remembering the dead he created in himself the notion of other forms of life, for which death is but the beginning and the conception of a life continuing after apparent death" (1993: 25; cf. *SE* 14: 294).

In the B'nai B'rith essay, in a passage cut from the *Imago* version, Freud provided a Jewish gloss, noting that the Holy Scriptures take no account of the afterlife, while popular Jewish religion takes a different stance on the doctrine of immortality. The entire passage is worth quoting:

> It is very remarkable that our Holy Scriptures have taken no
> account of this human need for a guarantee of continued existence.
> On the contrary, at one point it is said, "Only the living praise God."
> I believe — and you certainly know more about it than I do — that
> different stances have been taken on the doctrine of immortality in

popular Jewish religion and in the literature connected with the
Holy Scriptures. (27)

Freud continues to pursue the theme of immortality and Jewish-
Gentile difference in another passage present in the B'nai B'rith version
of the text, but absent from the *Imago* publication. He states that the
failure of Judaism to become a major world religion lay in its de-
emphasis of the doctrine of the afterlife: "I would like to include this
point too," he noted, "amongst those factors that prevented the Jewish
religion from taking the place of the other ancient religions after their
decline" (1993: 27–28). Judaism, in Freud's reading here, both embraces
and ignores immortality, as if a religion cannot have immortality unless
it promises immortality. The multilayered irony of this remark would
not have been lost upon this group. These Jews would have been quite
aware of the historical debates over the lack of a doctrine of immortality in Judaism.[15] They would have been quite conscious of being members of a group which had achieved a kind of immortality through its
very survival, without, in its canonical texts, promising a heavenly afterlife. They may have even feared or anticipated another, tragic dimension of this irony, the fact that a virulently anti-Semitic movement
would soon attempt to eliminate the "immortal" Jewish people entirely.

While Freud's remarks here do not develop fully the more complex
analysis of immortality and the afterlife we've encountered in other
texts, they are significant in locating the theme of immortality in the
context of passages addressed particularly to Jews and eliminated from
the more public text. Freud hints suggestively at an anatomy of the
problem of immortality "in Judaism" and "of Jewishness" in the face of
the forces of both anti-Semitism and assimilationism.

We have come to expect references to the absence of God in Freud's
texts associated with the uncanny — and here we are not disappointed.
The same misquoted reference to Shakespeare (*SE* 4: 205) discussed in
chapter 2 appears in this text, as well, as if to affirm the paradoxical
omnipresence of the absence of God in association with the uncanny

mother—and here, in association with Judaism, too. Freud offers his own reasoned assessment of the inevitability of death in a phrase which, as we noted previously, serves to displace God. Freud's words here, "each of us owes Nature his death" (1993: 12, *SE* 14: 289), eliminate the God Shakespeare placed in the text: "Thou owest God a death."

Freud also had quoted the Shakespearean line in a letter to Fliess in 1899 in a complex paragraph bemoaning the practice in "our modern medicine" of refusing to inform the terminally ill of their condition. In one of his few positive assessments of religion, he spoke of the honesty regarding death implicit in the Christian sacrament of last rites, linking the practice to Shakespeare's (misquoted) words and to his personal desire "when the time comes" to know the truth about his own death. He asked:

> What has the individual come to, how negligible must be the influence of the religion of science which is supposed to have taken the place of the old religion if one no longer dares to disclose that it is this or that man's turn to die? Breuer's spirit lives in these arts. The Christian at least has the last sacrament administered a few hours beforehand. And Shakespeare says, "Thou owest Nature a death." I hope that when my time comes I shall find someone who will treat me with greater respect and tell me when to be ready. My father was fully aware of it ... and retained his beautiful composure to the end. (Masson 1985: 343)

It is worth noting parenthetically that, according to his biographers, Freud was aware of and ready for the moment of his own death. It was he who told his daughter and his doctor that his "time had come."[16]

It is no accident that Freud associates in this epistolary paragraph the loss of "the old religion" and the religious practices associated with death, on the one hand, and on the other, the problematic "spirit of Breuer" and the "religion of science." In a sense, he foreshadows in the 1899 letter his later remarks in the B'nai B'rith address. The Shakespearean parapraxis links the passages across the years. Both eliminate

God, and both (through the anecdote and through references to the "spirit of Breuer," Freud's mentor and early collaborator, with whom he had had some conflicts shortly before writing this letter) reflect on a Jewish resistance to death. Thus, one of his few laudatory comments on Christianity contrasts Christian death rituals with Jewish (Breuer's) resistance to acknowledging death and with the denial of death in the "religion of science."

Here, Freud points toward, without fully developing, an analysis of the loss of God and religion in modernity. Shakespeare's words, made Godless by Freud, here as elsewhere are acclaimed for their acknowledgment of death. This Shakespearean death passage is associated with Christian sacramental practices which are not stripped of God. The denial of death versus the ability to embrace death, the presence of God versus the absence of God are the themes, Freud suggests, that Jews of his day encounter inevitably in their "post-colonial" situation (Boyarin 1994). And all these themes are closely intertwined with the uncanny.

Thus the lecture "Wir und der Tod," "Death and Us," addressed to a Jewish audience, links Jews and death, Jews and immortality, and Jewish mothers with deadly and dangerous refusals to obey the unconscious laws surrounding death. And it expresses the dangerous or deadly fear of Jewish assimilation into Gentile culture. All the elements of the uncanny appear in this text. And all these elements are removed from the more public version of the text. Freud's sense of his Jewishness clearly involves a sense of something "secret," *Geheim,* etymologically related, through *Heim,* "home," to the canny *heimlich* and the uncanny, *unheimlich.* The *Heimlichkeit* of Jewishness must remain an unspoken *Geheim* (secret) in an anti-Semitic world: the part of the text that identifies death with "us Jews" remains hidden from a broader public.

We have examined Freud's sense of the *Heimlichkeit* and *Unheimlichkeit* — the canniness and uncanniness — of his Jewish identity, finding that while Jewishness is *heimlich* to Freud the Jew, it is *unheimlich* to him at the same time. We have found that Freud's writings on the canniness of Jewishness to the Jew point toward a thesis distinctly different from his Oedipal masterplot. In this non-Oedipal thesis, Freud is not simply engaging in a hypermasculinization of Judaism. His attempt to re-envision the trope of the uncanny Jew as an uncanny maternal body, his attempt to articulate his sense of the *Heimlichkeit,* the "safe privacy of a common mental construction" among Jews (*SE* 20: 274), and his discussion of "death and us Jews" all contribute to an intellectual trajectory which he initiated, but was unable to complete. In this trajectory, Freud began to theorize the effects upon Jews of the attractions and dangers of Jewish assimilation into a dominant Gentile culture. These attractions and dangers, his counterthesis suggests, were closely connected to the dangerous and deadly mothers we encountered in his texts in chapter 2.

Further clues to the association of Jewishness with the uncanny mother lie in Freud's analysis of anti-Semitism and his comments on the bodily mark of Jewishness for the male, circumcision, which we shall encounter in the next chapter. Underlying the "uncanny impression" left by circumcision is a contradiction which is only apparent: both a fear of the female genitals and, to use the terminology of Julia Kristeva, a primal separation from the maternal "abject."

CHAPTER 4

The Sources
of Anti-Semitism

Circumcision, Abjection,
and the Uncanny Mother

Freud offered several analyses of the sources of anti-Semitism. In most of these, he assumed Oedipal conflicts to be at the root of anti-Semitic prejudices, focusing in particular on the castration fears evoked by circumcision. As we have seen in other contexts, however, Freud's analyses of castration anxiety often slip beyond the boundaries of the Oedipal framework. In this chapter, I examine Freud's interpretations of anti-Semitism, finding evidence of the counterthesis in his analysis of a common source for misogyny and anti-Semitism. This chapter turns from the *Heimlichkeit* of Jewish identity for the Jew to the *Unheimlichkeit,* the uncanniness or "Otherness" of Jewishness for the anti-Semite.

DEEPER MOTIVES FOR ANTI-SEMITISM

To speak of or to speak to the B'nai B'rith, the group to whom Freud spoke in his 1915 and 1926 addresses, was to evoke the male Jewish body: "B'nai B'rith" means "sons of the covenant." The sign of the covenant, of course, is circumcision. The name "B'nai B'rith" "evoked, for fin de siècle Viennese Jews, the image of circumcision" (Gilman 1993: 25). While Freud's seventieth-birthday address made circumcision part of the familiar, *heimlich,* common identity of male Jews, a later

99

text addressed to a broader audience describes circumcision explicitly as *unheimlich,* "uncanny." This later text, written in the 1930s, is *Moses and Monotheism.*

Although *Moses and Monotheism* is most explicitly an analysis of the history and character of the Jews, it is also an analysis of anti-Semitism. Jacques Le Rider notes that "some of the most interesting passages in *Moses and Monotheism* are devoted to outlining a theory of anti-semitism" (1993: 237). Freud himself, in a letter to Arnold Zweig, indicated that his purpose in the book was not only to analyze the development of the Jewish people, but also to understand anti-Semitism: "The starting point of my work is familiar to you . . . faced with the new persecutions, one asks oneself again how the Jews have come to be what they are and why they have attracted this undying hatred" (E. Freud 1970: 91). Freud answers in *Moses and Monotheism* that anti-Semitism is surely due to ancient and unconscious fears and fantasies: "The deeper motives for hatred of the Jews are rooted in the remotest past ages; they operate from the unconscious of the peoples."[1] Freud proposes two "deeper motives" for anti-Semitism, noting an expectation of resistance to his analysis of these motives: "I am prepared to find that at first they will not seem credible" (*SE* 23: 91).

The first motive, he suggests, is a kind of jealous rage over the chosenness of the Jews: "I venture to assert that jealousy of the people which declared itself the first born, favorite child of God the Father, has not yet been surmounted among other peoples even today. It is as though they had thought there was truth in the claim." This resentment, he goes on, reveals itself, upon further inspection, to be a kind of hostility toward an enforced monotheism in which hatred of Jews disguises a hostility toward Christianity among peoples whose religious sentiment is close to a "barbarous polytheism" (*SE* 23: 91). The second motive Freud enumerates is castration anxiety. Circumcision, he states, is uncanny, *unheimlich.* It evokes fears of castration: "Among the customs by which the Jews made themselves separate, that of circumcision has made a disagreeable, uncanny impression, which is to be explained, no doubt, by its recalling the dreaded castration and along with it a portion of the primeval past which is gladly forgotten" (*SE* 23: 91).

Freud's explanation of anti-Semitism in terms of an association of circumcision and castration seems relatively self-evident: it follows the metonymic logic of *pars pro toto*. While circumcision is "canny" to the Jew because it is the shared mark of a community, as the 1926 B'nai B'rith text implies, it is "uncanny" to the anti-Semite, as the 1930s text argues, because of castration anxiety. But this story of the (un)canny impression left by circumcision is not so simple. One must ask why Freud was "prepared to find" that his speculations would "not seem credible." Since he had explained anti-Semitism in terms of circumcision and castration anxiety in earlier texts (in footnotes to his Little Hans case and his essay on Leonardo), his expectation of an incredulous response requires explanation. A closer examination of these texts will show that the incompletely developed counterthesis emerging between the lines played a central role in producing his expectation of resistance to each of these references to circumcision and anti-Semitism.[2]

In a discussion of a childhood memory of Leonardo da Vinci's, the memory which gives Freud's 1910 essay its name, Freud recounts Leonardo's account of lying in his cradle when a bird — a vulture, in Freud's reading — descended, "opened my mouth with its tail and struck me many times with its tail against my lips" (*SE* 11: 82). In the process of interpreting, or misinterpreting, this memory (for Freud's interpretation of the bird as a vulture, we now know, was based, in part, on a mistranslation of Leonardo's text), Freud traces a complex set of associations. His journey takes the reader from Leonardo's memories of sucking at the breast of the mother (87), to homosexual fantasies of fellatio (86), to "virgin birth" or parthenogenesis among vultures (88–89), to androgynous Egyptian mother goddesses (88, 94), to the Christian doctrine of the virgin birth of Christ, to Leonardo's illegitimate birth (90), to phallic mothers, and finally to male infantile sexual theories about female genitals (95). Here we find the familiar Freudian analysis of the castration anxiety emerging when the male child "observes the genitals of little girls" (95). Freud's speculations on the male child's reaction to the sight of the genitals of the female child led him to an analysis of the source of misogyny, and — once again — to a reference to the *Unheimlichkeit* of the female genitals: "That the penis could be missing strikes him as an uncanny and intolerable idea . . . under the influence of this threat of castration. . . . Henceforth he will tremble for his masculinity, but at the same time he will despise the unhappy creatures on whom the cruel punishment has, as he supposes, already fallen" (95).[3] In other words, he suggests, in an argument similar to the one discussed earlier, that the origins of misogyny lie in castration anxiety and that the female genitals are uncanny to the male.

Freud returned to this passage nearly a decade later, in 1919, when he inserted a footnote linking misogyny and castration anxiety with anti-Semitism. "The conclusion strikes me as inescapable that here we may also trace one of the roots of the anti-semitism which appears with such elemental force and finds such irrational expression among the nations of the west. Circumcision is unconsciously equated with castration" (*SE* 11: 95–96 n. 1). Thus, a text on misogyny and the uncanniness of the female genitals is reread. In the new reading, this uncanniness becomes a clue to the riddle of anti-Semitism.

Why Freud added the footnote on anti-Semitism in 1919, or why he deferred an analysis of the intersections of anti-Semitism and misogyny for nearly a decade, represents one of the riddles of the text on Leonardo, particularly because he had made precisely the same connections a year prior to the publication of the Leonardo essay in a famous footnote to the 1909 Little Hans case history, "An Analysis of a Phobia in a Five-Year-Old Boy." Freud discusses in the 1909 text Little Hans's "enlightenment" *(Aufklärung)* regarding the fact that "women really do not possess a widdler *(wiwimacher)*." Hans's castration complex was aroused, he explains there: the child feared that "they could take his own widdler away and, as it were, make him into a woman" (*SE* 10:36). Adding a lengthy footnote to this text in 1909, Freud wrote,

I cannot interrupt the discussion so far as to demonstrate the typical character of the unconscious train of thought which I think there is here reason for attributing to Little Hans. The castration complex is the deepest unconscious root of anti-semitism; for even in the nursery little boys hear that a Jew has something cut off his penis — a piece of his penis, they think — and this gives them a right to despise Jews. And there is no stronger unconscious root for the sense of superiority over women. (*SE* 10: 36 n. 1)

In this footnote, Freud goes on to comment on the association of Jews and women within the perspective of a "neurotic" and "infantile complex," arguing that the neurotic fear of Jews and women can be traced to the castration complex.

Clear enough, so far. But a troubling passage in the center of this footnote exposes some "deeper motives" on Freud's part, raising questions about the internalization of anti-Semitism in the psyche of the Jew. Freud describes Otto Weininger's infamous *Sex and Character* as an illustration of the infantile and neurotic association of Jews and women. He states:

Weininger (the young philosopher who, highly gifted but sexually deranged, committed suicide after producing his remarkable book, *Geschlecht und Charakter* [1903]), in a chapter that attracted much attention, treated Jews and women with equal hostility and overwhelmed them with the same insults. Being a neurotic, Weininger was completely under the sway of his infantile complexes; and from that standpoint, what is common to Jews and women is their relation to the castration complex. (*SE* 10: 36 n. 1, parentheses and brackets in the original)

This passage has generated a large body of analytic literature in recent years. (See, for example, Le Rider 1993, Gilman 1993, Boyarin 1994, 1997, Geller 1997, 1999.) There are major differences in the interpretations of these scholars, but several have emphasized the fact that

Weininger and Little Hans were Jews, although they are not so identified in Freud's text. The Jewish identity of the figures who stand as illustrations of castration anxiety, misogyny, and anti-Semitism in this footnote, in other words, is obscured. Hans and Weininger both suffered from self-disgust or deep ambivalence about their Jewishness, an ambivalence which, these scholars argue, Freud shared, and which he endeavored to hide. Boyarin states, "by occluding the fact of Hans's Jewishness and by obscuring the role of his own here, Freud is hiding something" (1994: 37). Again we find that Jewishness and circumcision are not only *heimlich,* but also *unheimlich.* Boyarin finds in these remarks not only a theory of misogyny and anti-Semitism, but also an analysis of Jewish self-contempt: "We have in Freud's note on Little Hans not only an anatomy of misogyny and antisemitism — both read as products of the unconscious — but also of Jewish self-contempt, also read as a sort of inevitability" (Boyarin 1997: 237).

In a strikingly original analysis of these texts, Geller exposes the complex source of this footnote in Freud's symbolically adoptive relation to "Little Hans," now known to be Herbert Graf, the son of Freud's friend and colleague Max Graf. Geller shows that the child's father, concerned about the effects of an increasingly anti-Semitic Vienna, had considered raising his son as a Christian and that Freud had advised against this. Max Graf recalled that Freud had said to him: "If you do not let your son grow up as a Jew . . . you will deprive him of those sources of energy which cannot be replaced by anything else. . . . Do not deprive him of that advantage" (quoted in Geller 1999: 361–62). Geller proposes that as a consequence of Freud's advice, Graf did have his son circumcised and that the footnoted associations Freud would make between Little Hans's castration fear and circumcision are motivated by a set of complex factors: "By advising Max Graf upon the birth of his son, Freud had (god)fathered Herbert as a Jew; he acted as the *kvatter* (godfather) who hands the child over to the *mohel* (ritual circumciser) if not indeed assuming the paternal role of circumciser and binding Herbert to the tradition" (Geller 1999: 364). But Freud's paternal relation to Little Hans, unmentioned in the case study, is only one hidden factor recovered by Geller in this complex "family romance." Desperately desiring that Little Hans would become a strong, masculine Jew, Freud obscured his concern that Hans's behavior expressed homosexual fantasies. Thus, Geller shows, the footnote is deeply overdetermined: the Jewishness of the homosexual anti-Semite Weininger is suppressed, just as is the Jewishness of Little Hans, the child with homosexually tinged fantasies.

Other displacements are evident here, as well. Clearly, there is something missing or something deferred in Freud's speculations about anti-Semitism, misogyny, and circumcision anxiety in the Leonardo and Little Hans essays. Each text makes the insight marginal or liminal by relegating it to a footnote.[4] The Leonardo text makes the insight doubly marginal through a decade-long postponement, or, in Freud's terminology, *Nachträglichkeit* (deferral of action), before inscribing the thought in the published writings. The Little Hans text obscures the insight further by hiding or failing to acknowledge the Jewish identity and the potential homosexuality of Little Hans and the Jewish identity of the homosexual Weininger, not to mention the homosexual desires of Freud himself (Geller 1999, Boyarin 1997). In both of these passages, the analysis of misogyny as castration anxiety is close to — yet distant from — the analysis of anti-Semitism. The riddle of anti-Semitism and the riddle of misogyny are closely linked through circumcision and castration anxiety. Freud's footnoting of these associations and his decade-long delay of the extratextual reference serve at the same time to acknowledge and to defer an association of the woman, the Jew, and the homosexual uncannily haunting the texts.[5]

In *Moses and Monotheism,* the text with which we began this discussion of the uncanniness of circumcision, Freud located his analysis of anti-Semitism centrally within the text itself, rather than in footnotes, but he excised what was earlier central to his extratextual analysis: misogyny. While in "Leonardo" and the Little Hans case he used circumcision and castration anxiety to speculate on the origins of hostility both to Jews and to women, he omitted any explicit reference to women in *Moses and Monotheism*. Yet, although the passage on circumcision in *Moses and Monotheism* does not refer to misogyny, an analysis of the misogynist ideologies of female inferiority and difference lie below the surface, pointing toward the incompletely articulated counterthesis.

Freud stated in *Moses and Monotheism* that circumcision itself is a *leitfossil,* a leading, guiding, or characteristic fossil, a "key-fossil" in Strachey's translation, which provides hints to the solution to the riddle of anti-Semitism and the riddle of Judaism. Freud wrote, for example, "we may once again call on the evidence afforded by circumcision, which has repeatedly been of help to us, like, as it were, a key-fossil" (*SE* 23: 39; cf. Geller 1993). Freud's use of the term *leitfossil* in relation to circumcision is not insignificant. It resonates with the analysis of the uncanny we discussed in chapters 2 and 3. As we saw earlier, the uncanny often involves the fear of being buried alive — not unlike the ancient fossils, evidence of the earth's living past, which had so fascinated the nineteenth-century European world. If circumcision is a fossil, then Judaism, to Freud, is a fossil as well: "From the 'triumph of Christianity' . . . the Jewish religion was to some extent a fossil" (*SE* 23: 88). The entire tradition of Judaism, he implies, has been uncannily buried alive (Geller 1993: 54). Again Freud's metaphors expose unconscious chains of associations linking circumcision and the uncanny. Metaphors related to the uncanny even appear in Freud's comments on the book itself. In the process of writing *Moses and Monotheism,* Freud noted self-reflexively, the book "tormented me like an unlaid ghost" (*SE* 23: 103), refusing, as it were, a premature, uncanny burial.

As noted in a previous chapter, the final pages of Freud's essay "The Uncanny" described three sites of the uncanny. The sense of the uncanny, he states, emerges with the thought of castration, the thought of being buried alive, and the thought of the mother's genitals. In *Moses and Monotheism,* in his explanation of anti-Semitism as a form of castration anxiety, he alludes to precisely the same set of images he had earlier used to illustrate the uncanny: he describes a "disagreeable, uncanny impression" created by circumcision, he explains that uncanny impression as a result of the fear of "the dreaded castration," and in a distorted image of burial, he refers to circumcision as a "fossil" and to castration as "a portion of the primeval past which is gladly forgotten."

In a distorted or deferred way, then, Freud associated woman and Jew or misogyny and anti-Semitism in *Moses and Monotheism* in a set of fragmentary remarks which not only reflect the racist and sexist ideologies of his world, the "traumatic knowledge" of the cultural equation of woman and Jew (Geller 1993: 52, 60), but also point toward an incomplete analysis of the sources of anti-Semitism in association with misogyny.

Thus, what Freud feared would "not seem credible" in his analysis of anti-Semitism was something that even he was able to articulate only in oblique references: an association of both Judaism and anti-Semitism with the uncanny and its accompaniments, that is, the ideology of dangerous and deadly female or maternal difference. Freud moved toward but stopped short of a full articulation of a theory in which anti-Semitism, misogyny, and circumcision/castration anxiety reside in the space of the unspeakable, uncanny body of the mother. Although Freud showed the way hesitantly toward this territory, Julia Kristeva has mapped the terrain with greater precision. A Kristevan reading of Judaism, anti-Semitism, and circumcision in terms of the "abject" therefore exposes more clearly the counterthesis that Freud was attempting to articulate.

A KRISTEVAN CARTOGRAPHY OF THE ABJECT

Before discussing Julia Kristeva's theory of the abject, it may be useful to return to Freud's analysis of the "deeper motives" for anti-Semitism. As noted above, Freud proposed two sources of anti-Semitism: one was the "uncanny impression" made by circumcision, the other was the jealous rage over the chosenness of the Jews. Lest this second source be interpreted as a kind of sibling rivalry, Freud quickly elaborated that this jealousy is a deflection of a deeper resentment against the enforced imposition of the monotheistic law. Contrary to typical expectations, he explained, anti-Semitism in its current forms is not a particularly or uniquely Christian pathology. Rather, noting that fascism opposes all forms of monotheism, he suggested that anti-Semitism is a kind of infantile anti-Christianity in which hostility toward Christianity is displaced, deflected, or projected outward as hostility toward Judaism:

> We must not forget that all those peoples who excel to-day in their hatred of Jews became Christians only in late historic times, often driven to it by bloody coercion. It might be said that they are all "misbaptized". They have been left, under a thin veneer of Christianity, what their ancestors were, who worshipped a barbarous polytheism. They have not got over a grudge against the new religion which was imposed on them; but they have displaced the grudge on to the source from which Christianity reached them. . . . Their hatred of Jews is at bottom a hatred of Christians, and we need not be surprised that in the German National-Socialist revolution this intimate relation between the two monotheist religions finds such a clear expression in the hostile treatment of both of them. (*SE* 23: 91–92)

Although he was rarely favorably disposed toward Christianity, Freud suggests here that the antistructural rage against the authority of God the Father and the chosenness of the Jews evident in National Socialism cannot be simply described as a Christian form of jealousy over the relation of a father toward the first born and best loved. In spite of the fact that *Moses and Monotheism* challenges Roman Catholic Christianity — see, for example, Freud's remarks on his hesitation about publishing the earliest versions of the text for fear of exposing psychoanalysis to the hostility of the Roman Catholic Church (*SE* 23: 55–57) — he does not simply hold Christianity responsible for anti-Semitism. Instead, he emphasizes the fact that Aryan ideology expresses a form of hostility toward monotheism in both its Christian and Jewish forms.

Freud's discussion of the "deeper motives" for anti-Semitism is remarkably similar to the analysis of anti-Semitism developed by the French-Bulgarian poststructuralist psychoanalyst Julia Kristeva in *Powers of Horror.* Kristeva devotes nearly half of *Powers of Horror* to the problem of anti-Semitism. Two aspects of her analysis are particularly striking. First, without any explicit reference to *Moses and Monotheism,* Kristeva develops an analysis that closely parallels Freud's. Second, her analysis exposes a theoretical perspective that lies between the lines and under the surface of Freud's text: the psychological proximity of misogyny to anti-Semitism (Jonte-Pace 1997a, 1999b). Using the texts of the twentieth-century French novelist and pamphleteer Louis-Ferdinand Céline as exemplary and paradigmatic anti-Semitic documents, Kristeva develops an interpretation of the psychological foundations of anti-Semitism. She argues that Céline's anti-Semitic discourses expose the skeletal framework of the social and political realities of the time: his words "present us with harsh X-rays of given *areas* of social and political experience" (1982: 177).

Like Freud, who discovered two "deeper motives," Kristeva discovers "two common features" (178) in anti-Semitism. The first is a rage against Judaism interpreted as an embodiment of the institutional structures of law, mastery, and society — the "register" which she, following Lacan, calls "Mastery" or the "Symbolic." This, she writes, is a *"rage against the Symbolic,* represented here by religious, para-religious, and moral establishments . . . it culminates in what Céline hallucinates and knows to be their foundation and forebear — Jewish monotheism" (178).

This "hatred of Mastery," Kristeva argues, embodies a rage against the religion of the father and the law: "At this far point of 'delirium' the anti-Semite unveils his denied but fierce belief in the Absolute of Jewish Religion as religion of the Father and of the Law; the anti-Semite is its possessed servant . . . who provides *a contrario* proof of monotheistic power of which he becomes the symptom, the failure, the envier" (184–85). Thus, anti-Semitism can be traced in part to a resistance to monotheistic mastery or a rage against the law of the father. Kristeva adds that twentieth-century anti-Semitism cannot be understood as a Christian pathology: to the anti-Semite, it is "Judeo-Christian monotheism" that represents "a fulfillment of religion as sacred horror" (210). Christianity is resisted, rejected, and raged against, alongside Judaism, as another form of "the Symbolic." Thus Kristeva and Freud, in arguments remarkably similar, both emphasize in anti-Semitism the rage and resentment evoked by the one God and His law. Both emphasize the significance of a paradoxical anti-Christianism alongside the hatred of the Jew.

Kristeva's deeper interest, however, is in the second feature of anti-Semitic ideology, a fantasy of a "Jewish threat" emanating from what is excluded from mastery or the symbolic. She states, "the second is the attempt to substitute *another Law* for the constraining and frustrating symbolic one" (178). She continues, "the image of the Jew will concentrate negated love become hatred for Mastery on the one hand, and on the other and jointly, desire for what mastery cuts out: weakness, the joying substance, sex tinged with femininity and death" (180). This is the territory of what Kristeva calls "the abject."

The "abject" is the central focus of *The Powers of Horror.* The notion of the "abject" provides a foundation for Kristeva's theory of religion. She describes a primitive terror of maternal engulfment that threatens the boundaries of the self almost before those boundaries come into being. As the Kristevan theorist Cleo Kearns explains, abjection "afflicts a troubled and unformed entity that knows itself as an I only through the sense of having been thrown out or repulsed from an other" (Kearns 1993: 58). The abject can be experienced in the loathing one feels for rotting food, filth, or excrement, defilement, muck, pus, and decay. It is not unrelated to the fear of death or of the corpse. It is the psychological foundation, Kristeva suggests, for religious concepts of sin, impurity, and pollution. To speak of it is to begin to speak of the unspeakable. It is the other side of the sacred: "As Abjection — So the Sacred" (1982: 17).

According to Kristeva, "Abjection accompanies all religious structurings and reappears, to be worked out in a new guise, at the time of their collapse" (1982: 17). Anti-Semitism is precisely this: a contemporary mask for abjection. Describing the Aryan mentality, she asks:

> Is not this dreaded Jew an object of the Father, a piece of waste, his wife as it were, an abjection? . . . an unbearable conjoining of the One and the Other, of Law and Jouissance . . . anti-Semitic fantasy relegates that object to the place of the ab-ject. The Jew: a conjunction of waste and object of desire, of corpse and life, fecality and pleasure . . . becomes the feminine exalted to the point of mastery. (185)

She links this explicitly with the maternal: "'something maternal' happens to bear upon the uncertainty that I call abjection" (208).

Kristeva extends this analysis further, arguing that the Jew "precipitates" these fantasies, that in a certain respect, the anti-Semite "is not mistaken" (186), that in anti-Semitic discourse, "there emerge a few striking words of truth" (177): "The anti-Semite is not mistaken. Jewish monotheism is not only the most rigorous application of Unicity of the Law and the Symbolic; it is also the one that wears with the greatest assurance, but like a lining, the mark of maternal, feminine, or pagan substance . . . *a scription on the limits of identity comes face to face with abjection*" (186, italics in the original).

Her remarks must not be misinterpreted. By no means does she condone anti-Semitism. Rather, she attempts to analyze and understand the psychological dynamics by which Jewish monotheism enrages and horrifies, the mechanisms by which the law and what the law excludes elicit rage and horror. Kristeva's attempt to gaze in the face of horror is remarkably similar to Freud's unwaveringly analytic stance in relation to the horror or *Grauen* he analyzes in so many of the texts examined here. Most significantly, both Freud and Kristeva (Kristeva more openly than Freud) point toward a theory of anti-Semitism in close proximity to the body of the mother. Kristeva's theory of the abject and Freud's counterthesis are closely related. Both are attempts to speak the unspeakable.

For Kristeva, religious rituals are attempts to establish boundaries around the abject protecting "the Symbolic" from the pollution or chaos embodied by the abject. In her analysis, rituals maintain and repair broken or threatened barriers between the sacred, safe, clean *(propre)* world of the symbolic, and the polluted, unclean territory of the abject, which is closely associated with the feminine and maternal. Thus, rituals attempt to differentiate an abject, maternal chaos from an orderly, symbolic cosmos.

Not only does Kristeva link anti-Semitism specifically with misogyny through an analysis of the abjection underlying xenophobia, but she also suggests that circumcision itself, to the Jew as well as to the anti-Semite, involves unconscious fears of the unnameable abject. In *Powers of Horror,* she introduces the problem of phobia by recalling Freud's analysis of Little Hans. Describing Little Hans's fear of horses, she asks what Hans really fears. Freud, she notes, "detects the fear of castration" (34). This, she argues is "astonishingly true, and not quite so" (34). The phobia of horses becomes a "hieroglyph that condenses all fears . . . a metaphor of want as such" (34–35).

Kristeva's chapter titles lay out the itinerary followed by her analysis of these fears condensed in Little Hans's phobia. "Something to be Scared Of" (32) leads "From Filth to Defilement" (56), that is, from castration fear, to the horror of the abject. From the abject and its source in the terror of maternal engulfment, the analysis arrives at the "Semiotics of Biblical Abomination" (90), via the intersection of "sublimation and perversion" in religion (89) and particularly in the ritual of circumcision. Thus, Kristeva's analysis proceeds from Freud to the Bible in three steps outlining a circle: she moves from the meaning of Little Hans's castration anxiety, to the horror of the abject, to circumcision rituals in Leviticus. Although castration and circumcision are the beginning and end of her analysis, it is not the circumcised penis around which her analysis pivots. Rather, it is the body of the mother. For Kristeva, circumcision is a way of separating a fragile self from the body of the mother, and castration anxiety is an echo of what might be called "abjection anxiety."

Central to her analysis of the biblical laws of purity and holiness is the discussion of circumcision in relation to the uncleanness of women after parturition in Leviticus 12. Kristeva recites the biblical text: because of the process of childbirth and the blood accompanying it, according to Leviticus 12: 2, the woman is impure: "According to the days of separation for her infirmity shall she be unclean." If she gives birth to a daughter, she "shall be unclean two weeks, as in her separation" (Leviticus 12: 5). Purification is enacted through sacrifice: the mother must provide a burnt offering and a sin offering. On the other hand, if she gives birth to a male, "the flesh of his foreskin shall be circumcised" (Leviticus 12: 3). Circumcision of the male child replaces the sacrifice needed in the case of the female child. Circumcision separates the male child from maternal impurity and defilement. It is equivalent to sacrifice as "a sign of the alliance with God" (99).

In Kristeva's reading, Leviticus 12 is a text concerning "feminine and particularly maternal impurity" which articulates the notion that "what the male is separated from, the other that circumcision carves out on his very sex, is the other sex, impure, defiled." She notes a parallel between the navel and the circumcised penis: "By repeating the natural scar of the umbilical cord at the location of sex, by duplicating and thus displacing through ritual the preeminent separation, which is that from the mother, Judaism seems to insist in symbolic fashion ... that the identity of the speaking being (with his God) is based on the separation of the son from the mother" (99–100).[6]

Although in Kristeva's analysis circumcision as ritual represents a separation from the feminine or maternal abject, it never leaves the abject fully behind: the scars of circumcision provide a lasting reminder of the missing piece and its symbolism, a kind of doubling of the symbolism of the navel which marks the male as twice separated from the mother. Thus, a Kristevan reading identifies circumcision as a marker dividing the abject from the symbolic. Circumcision identifies the male infant as part of a male patrilineage, born first into abjection from the biological body of the mother, reborn out of abjection by means of the social body of fathers and their symbolic actions. Circumcision thus separates the male child from his prior identity, from his birth by a physical mother (see Eilberg-Schwartz 1990, Jay 1992). A Kristevan analysis of abjection uncovers another layer in the fears and fantasies toward which Freud pointed in his reading of the common origins of anti-Semitism and misogyny.

By locating the origins of anti-Semitism and misogyny in castration anxiety, Freud developed a theory in which the practice of circumcision is central to the hostility toward Jews. Kristeva's analysis also finds an anxiety generated by circumcision central to anti-Semitism, but in her reading, the original anxiety is not castration anxiety, but rather the horror of the abject. Circumcision is secondary: the separation inscribed by circumcision is a reiteration of the earlier separation from the maternal abject. The ritual of circumcision separates the circumcised male from the abject, but the anti-Semite collapses the categories. Circumcision and Jewishness stand in for the horrifying maternal abject. While Freud believed that castration anxiety was the deepest form of anxiety, Kristeva shows that the horror of the abject lies deeper, and that castration anxiety emerges as a later manifestation of the horror, or *Grauen,* of maternal abjection. Freud's goal was to explain anti-Semitism in particular. Kristeva's theory, although also focused on the "mind of the anti-Semite," offers as well an analysis of xenophobia in general.[7]

RETURNING TO FREUD

What Freud was able to acknowledge in 1909 and 1919 only in footnotes, and what he could articulate only implicitly and between the lines in the 1930s, has thus been described explicitly by Julia Kristeva. Where Freud was a hesitant, cautious, or circumspect analyst of the intersections of misogyny and anti-Semitism, Kristeva is a bolder analyst of these intersections. Her insights extend and clarify Freud's analysis, serving to press Freud's interpretations into dialogue with feminist and post-structuralist insights. Her analyses of abjection originate, she herself acknowledges, at the same source from which "Freud had caught a glimpse: the gushing forth of the unconscious, the repressed, suppressed pleasure, be it sex or death" (206).[8] Kristeva finds the sources of anti-Semitism within the same territories Freud located them: in the rage against the monotheistic law of the father and in the fear of the feminine or maternal space of abjection and abhorrence. As we have seen, her particular interest, like his, was in the second source. Her "abject" is close to his "uncanny." Both theorists discovered this to be a maternal space, and both found it vitally important, as Kristeva puts it, to tear "the veil of the communitarian mystery, on which love of self and others is set up, only to catch a glimpse of the abyss of abjection within which they are underlaid" (209). The analyses of both Freud and Kristeva help to expose the psychological dynamics of the connections between anti-Semitism and misogyny and the effects of an ideology positing the female and the Jew as Other. Kristeva aids us in uncovering some of the incompletely articulated insights in Freud's counterthesis exploring the uncanniness of Jewishness both to the xenophobe and to the Jew.[9]

Kristeva's work makes possible a deeper inquiry into Freud's psychoanalytic theory of culture by supporting Freud's cautious, deferred, and forgotten speculations regarding the common space of anti-Semitism and misogyny. By reading Freud's cultural texts alongside the work of Kristeva, we can begin to see new possibilities for psychoanalytic theory — possibilities that Freud himself was unable to articulate fully. In this reading, Freud emerges clearly as a critic of cultural misogyny, anti-Semitism, and xenophobia (Jonte-Pace 1999b: 29, 30) and as a participant in the project of "feminist analysis."

Previous chapters have shown that an incompletely articulated theory of unconscious associations of maternity, mortality, and immortality — a non-Oedipal counterthesis — can in fact be found in Freud's texts. We have seen evidence of this counterthesis in Freud's descriptions of his own *heimlich* Jewish identity, in his analysis of the *Unheimlichkeit* of the Jew to the anti-Semite, in his writings on the *unheimlich* mother, and in his interpretations of the religious belief in the *Heimlichkeit* of the afterlife. There remains another site where this counterthesis is evident: Freud's writings on mourning and melancholia. While Freud was a successful mourner of lost religion, he was an unsuccessful or "melancholic" mourner of the mother. In spite of this, and in spite of his inability to theorize the interrelations of maternity, mortality, and immortality, however, the unspun threads of his counterthesis nevertheless contain hints of a fuller tapestry which might help us understand the difficulties of living in modernity — and the possibilities of living without misogyny and xenophobia.

CHAPTER 5

Modernity, Melancholia, and the (In)Ability to Mourn

When Throne and Altar Are in Danger

In "Fetishism," written just as he was finishing *The Future of an Illusion,* his most famous critique of religion, Freud addresses one of his favorite themes: the adamant denial of the male child in the first encounter with sexual difference. Here, he links the child's anxious and defensive response with the panic of the adult male whose political and religious structures are endangered. In spite of having seen the nude body of the mother, Freud suggests, a young boy refuses "to take cognizance of the fact of his having perceived that a woman does not possess a penis." The child imagines, in Freud's reconstruction, "No, that could not be true: for if a woman had been castrated then his own possession of a penis was in danger." Speculating further, Freud proposes, "in later life a grown man may perhaps experience a similar panic when the cry goes up that Throne and Altar are in danger" (*SE* 21: 153).

The endangered "Throne and Altar" in Freud's reading, of course, are cultural institutions whose instability evokes castration anxiety. Painting a vivid picture with a few simple verbal strokes, Freud portrays throne and altar as fragile stand-ins for the phallus, at risk through the mere presence of the one whose phallus is perceived as absent: the woman/mother. His analysis exposes the phallocentrism of politics, law, and religion, and the misogyny intertwined with castration anxiety arising when those structures are challenged. In Freud's analysis, which anticipates later feminist cultural theory, both the stability and the fragility of religion and society are gendered. Unconscious misogyny amplifies or underlies the state of panic over religious and social instability. Freud may well have been ruminating here about the possible effects of his own work in promoting religious and social instability, castration anxiety, and misogyny. He had started *The Future of an Illusion,* with its many-pronged attack on religious belief and morality, just a few months prior to writing these words about thrones and altars, and he completed it just weeks afterward.[1]

THRONE, ALTAR, AND MISOGYNIST PANIC

Let us turn to one of Freud's analyses of dangers to "Thrones" and "Altars" written in 1915, a short essay called "On Transience." "On Transience" was written at the same time as his better known metapsychological essay "Mourning and Melancholia." In both these texts, Freud discusses the response to instability, transience, and loss. Peter Homans calls the writings of 1915 Freud's "protocultural texts," suggesting that they "body forth the central problems and ideas of the better-known cultural texts" (1989: 196). Homans's view is quite accurate. Many of the insights of the 1915 texts were developed further in Freud's later analyses of religion and culture. The connection between the 1915 analyses of loss and mourning and the 1927 remarks on the panic arising when the "cry goes up that Throne and Altar are in danger" is just one example of such insights. Many of these point suggestively toward the counterthesis undergirding Freud's inquiries into unconscious reactions to the death and loss of beloved people and valued ideals.

In 1915, Freud wrote several texts on death, loss, and mourning. These include the lecture discussed in the preceding chapter, "Death and Us," which he presented to the B'nai B'rith, the revision and expansion of that lecture published in *Imago* in 1916 as part of "Thoughts for the Times on War and Death," the famous metapsychological essay

"Mourning and Melancholia," drafted in 1915 and published two years later, and a short composition for the Berlin Goethe Society, "On Transience." These are sets of companion texts. As chapter 3 suggests, "Thoughts for the Times on War and Death" can be read alongside the B'nai B'rith lecture "Death and Us" as a way of differentiating the public Freud, the scientist and universalist, from the private Freud — the Jew. Similarly, "On Transience" can be read alongside "Mourning and Melancholia." The latter is the more public, theoretical analysis of loss. "On Transience" is a personal reflection, framed within a narrative context, addressing the same themes.

"Mourning and Melancholia" and "On Transience" reflect Freud's careful observations of his own conscious and unconscious processes during a period of anticipated and actual loss. These texts are intricately overdetermined. Both were written as Freud approached his sixtieth year, when, as we have seen, he believed that he had only a year or two to live. They were written shortly after his break with Jung, an experience of disillusionment and loss nearly equivalent to a death.[2] They were written during World War I, a war unprecedented in its ferocity and destruction, a war during which Freud feared for the survival of his two sons at the front and for the survival of psychoanalysis itself. In addition, these texts were written during the period Le Rider calls the "modern crisis of culture," when codes of gender identity and religious identity in Vienna had undergone dramatic shifts. These texts represent both a documentation of a period of mourning and loss — including a de-idealization of strongly held values — and a profound meditation on that process of loss. They represent analyses of dangers to "Throne and Altar," as well as of dangers to beloved people and ideals.

Like "Mourning and Melancholia," "On Transience" offers an analysis of the human response to death, loss, and change. Each text outlines two distinct reactions to loss: a form of grief leading to mourning and recovery and a pathological variant of mourning — paradoxically involving a refusal to mourn — remaining unnamed in "On Transience," but called "melancholia" in the other essay. Juxtaposing these two texts is instructive. Freud articulated in "On Transience" some important additions to the theory he presented in "Mourning and Melancholia." The two texts, read together, contain an insightful analysis of how mourning and melancholia happen, what depression feels like, how the pain of loss influences the ego, how pain diminishes over time, how new "structures" replace lost loves and ideals, and how mourning and melancholia differ. Like "Death and Us," "On Transience" reflects concerns with Jewish identity, assimilation, and anti-Semitism. In addition, it contains subtle reflections on the uncanny mother. "On Transience" serves to link "Mourning and Melancholia" with the complex of ideas we have traced in earlier chapters: maternity, mortality, and immortality, Jewishness and anti-Semitism.

In "Mourning and Melancholia," Freud examines the similarities and differences between the usual process of grieving or mourning *(Trauer)* and the more intense, painful, and pathological variant of mourning, known to the medical community of his era as melancholia, which was similar to what is called clinical depression today. Both, he argued, originate with the death or loss of a loved object or ideal: they are "reactions to the loss of a loved person or to the loss of some abstraction" *(SE* 14: 243). In both, the subject experiences a painful "withdrawal of the libido from the object" (249).

Melancholia, he argues, differs from mourning in several ways. First, it involves a deep ambivalence in the relationship to the loved object. The lost object is both loved and hated: "Countless separate struggles are carried on over the object in which love and hate contend with each other" (256). Second, this ambivalence is internalized in a struggle which results in a dual or conflicted sense of self and a loss of self-esteem, an "extraordinary diminution in . . . self-regard" (246). Third, while in mourning "there is nothing about the loss that is unconscious," melancholia can involve "an object loss which is withdrawn from consciousness" (245). Fourth, while mourning is typically a reaction to a specific loss, often due to a death, melancholia may be a result of a less specific sense of loss, including a sense of fragmentation from having been "slighted, neglected, or disappointed" many times (251). Fifth, hinting at the notion of the death instinct which he would develop more clearly a few years later, Freud noted that melancholia "overcomes the instinct which compels every living thing to cling to life" (246), and, at the same time, it involves an intense fear of death. Finally, the pain associated with mourning comes to an end, but the pain of melancholia is extended endlessly. Freud explains that while mourning lasts, it

> absorbs all the energies of the ego. . . . Each single one of the memories and situations of expectancy which demonstrate the libido's attachment to the lost object is met by the verdict of reality that the object no longer exists; and the ego, confronted as it were with the question whether it shall share this fate, is persuaded by the sum of the narcissistic satisfactions it derives from being alive to sever its attachment to the object that has been abolished. (Phillips 1999: 122–23; cf. Freud *SE* 14: 245, 255)[3]

In addition to the severing of the attachment, Freud describes a process in which the lost object is internalized and new psychic structures are "built up." In melancholia, on the other hand, the libido continuously flows out as if through "an open wound" (253). The attachment is not severed, the loss is not internalized, and the building of new psychic structures is obstructed. While mourning and melancholia, in Freud's analysis, share many elements, melancholia can be said to be an extreme, protracted, or pathological form of mourning.

Freud described mourning as the healthier, preferred, or normative response to loss, yet he occasionally privileged melancholia. Melancholics, for example, are said to have remarkable abilities to understand the self, the other, and the world. The melancholic, whose self-opinion Freud compared to Hamlet's, has a "keener eye for the truth than other people" and "has come pretty near to understanding himself" (246). Reflecting a widespread trope in the Western literary and philosophical tradition of the melancholy, but insightful soul (Schiesari 1992), Freud ponders, "we only wonder why a man has to be ill before he can be accessible to a truth of this kind" (246). By describing the melancholic in terms of his "keener eye for the truth," Freud, who surely saw himself as one with a keen eye for truth, expresses a partial and subtle identification with the melancholic. This tension between the preferred path of the healthy mourner and the wise, self-knowing, unhealthy melancholic is an echo of the tension between masterplot and counterthesis.[4]

"On Transience" is a short essay composed at the request of the Berlin Goethe Society for a commemorative volume issued in 1916, *Das Land Goethes* (Goethe's country). This "elaborately produced volume" (Strachey, in Freud *SE* 14: 304) contained contributions from well-known artists, writers, and poets. In his contribution to the volume, Freud discussed, less systematically but more poetically and dramatically, the same material he had presented in "Mourning and Melancholia." Here he framed an analysis of reactions to loss within what was not just a personal narrative, but an account of a cultural tragedy. In addition he elaborated upon the melancholic reaction to loss, without actually using the term *melancholia,* by introducing the themes of the refusal to mourn and the demand for immortality. In this essay, he clearly privileged mourning over melancholia. He sympathetically but unambiguously critiqued the melancholic response to loss. And he referred, albeit indirectly, to the tensions between assimilationism and traditionalism for Jews in Germanic culture.

Appropriately enough, Freud begins the essay for a volume on Goethe's country with an idyllic memory of a lovely stroll through the countryside: "Not long ago, I went on a summer walk through a smiling countryside in the company of a taciturn friend and of a young but already famous poet" (14: 305). The idyll was quickly disturbed: Freud's friends found themselves unable to feel pleasure in the beauty of the landscape. The poet "admired the beauty of the scene," but "felt no joy in it." Freud offers an interpretation of the poet's lack of joy: disturbed "by the thought that all this beauty was fated to extinction . . . all that he would otherwise have loved and admired seemed to him to be shorn of its worth by the transience which was its doom" (305).

Suggesting that "the idea that all this beauty was transient was giving these two sensitive minds a foretaste of mourning over its decease," he describes the reaction of his friends as a "revolt . . . against mourning" and a "demand for immortality" (*SE* 14: 306, 305). He adds a preliminary interpretation: "Since the mind instinctively recoils from anything that is painful, they felt their enjoyment of beauty interfered with by thoughts of its transience" (*SE* 14: 305–6). Transience is thus opposed to immortality.

This description of the rejection of transience, the demand for immortality, and the revolt against mourning, while remaining consistent with "Mourning and Melancholia," extends the analysis Freud had written a few months earlier. In this scenario, the troubled friends experience a withdrawal of libido from the object (the countryside), a premature, anticipatory grief, a grief connected to a nonspecific loss that was not a death, and an insistence on the immortality or *Unsterblichkeit* of the object. Without naming their malady, Freud describes his friends with symptoms close to those he diagnosed as melancholia in the metapsychological text. An identification of the sensitive poet as melancholic reflects the tradition recounted by Schiesari in *The Gendering of Melancholia* (1992) of the *Dichter,* the poet or writer who perceives deeper truths, but cannot find joy in the outside world.

Shifting the narrative from his friends' melancholic impasse in the revolt against mourning, Freud offers his own view as a superior alternative to that of his colleagues. Here he lauds the reasonable path of the good mourner. While the young poet and the taciturn friend experienced a "revolt in their minds against mourning" (*SE* 14: 306), refusing to grieve and refusing to acknowledge the presence of loss, change, and death in life, Freud himself mourned: he accepted "the transience of all things" and disputed the poet's view that the "transience of what is beautiful involves any loss in its worth." The impermanence of beauty, and of life itself, should neither diminish the beauty nor obstruct our experience of pleasure. It is incomprehensible "that the thought of the transience of beauty should interfere with our joy in it" (305). The inevitability of death and loss, in Freud's view, increases the value of the objects we love. To experience this is to be able to mourn. The ability to mourn makes possible the ability to love, to feel pleasure, to enjoy beauty.

In his narrative account of his walk through the countryside with the refusers of mourning, Freud informed his readers that he himself maintained his ability to mourn even in the face of direct personal and cultural loss and disillusionment. He situated his account of the walk with the poet and the presentation of his theory of transience in the context of the war occurring in Europe as he wrote the essay: "My conversation with the poet took place in the summer before the war. A year later war broke out.... It destroyed not only the beauty of the countryside through which it passed ... but it also shattered our pride in the achievements of our civilization ... and our hopes of a final triumph over the differences between nations and races" (307). The war led, in other words, to a dramatic encounter with the transience of valued objects and ideals. While deeply saddened by the loss of all he valued, Freud remained hopeful. Grieving over all that had perished, he noted that the period of mourning would eventually end. He looked forward to the cessation of mourning and the subsequent creation of new achievements, structures, and ideals: "When once the mourning is over ... we shall build up again all that war has destroyed, and perhaps on firmer ground and more lastingly than before" (14: 307).

The dashed hopes of a final triumph over "differences between nations and races" included the hope for an end to tensions between German and Jew. Writing to the Gentile readers of the Goethe Society's volume, Freud expressed the assimilationist desire to maintain an enlightened or rational sense of Jewish identity while, at the same time, unreservedly accepting Germanic culture (see Le Rider 1993: 205). Freud honored the best of the dominant culture through this homage to Goethe, this essay for *Das Land Goethes*. His analysis of the tensions between his own position and the reactions of his hiking companions can be read as an account of the tensions between anti-assimilationist and assimilationist desires. This point deserves further explanation.

One of his companions on the summer walk through the smiling countryside, the Dolomites, was either Sandor Ferenczi or Karl Abraham — both Jews, both part of the psychoanalytic movement. Both had joined the Freud family for a few days in August 1913 (Strachey *SE* 14: 305; Jones 1955: 113). The Gentiles in Freud's circle were Jones and Jung. Neither were poets, and neither walked through the countryside with him in the summer of 1913. The other companion, whose name and whose malady remain unidentified, was, in all likelihood, a Jew as well.[5]

Without identifying these terms or characters directly, Freud recounts in "On Transience" a story of "wandering Jews" in Goethe's country. Relevant here are his 1915 remarks to the B'nai B'rith discussed in the preceding chapter regarding the attitude toward death revealed "most frequently and in the most extreme ways" by "us Jews" (Freud 1993: 11). In "On Transience," he contrasts the melancholic Jews (his companions) with the mourning Jew (himself). The melancholic companions demand immortality (of the land, of the religion), while the mourning Jew takes the rationalist position, which is also an assimilationist position. He acknowledges the loss of the land and the loss of the traditional religion. Although I suggested that in "Mourning and Melancholia" Freud situated himself as both mourner and melancholic, here Freud is unambiguously the mourner, the assimilated Jew. His essay acknowledges that the land is Germanic *(Das Land Goethes)* and that the Jews walking through Goethe's smiling countryside are, in a sense, wandering Jews, "uncanny," *unheimlich* Jews, who are not "at home," *heimlich,* in Goethe's country. His colleagues are unable to mourn and unable to assimilate: they are beset by what he elsewhere called melancholia.

This essay works on many levels. Explicitly, Freud's focus is the reaction to the thought of the seasonal loss of the countryside's beauty, which he links directly to the loss of life, land, and ideals in war. Underlying his discussion of these losses are his reactions to the loss of Jewish tradition demanded by assimilationism. Freud's recent painful break with Jung — and the loss of his hopes that the Gentile Jung would play a central role in communicating psychoanalytic ideas to a Gentile and potentially anti-Semitic audience — underlies this text as well. The devastation caused by the war is an apt metaphor for the devastation caused by Jung's defection from the psychoanalytic movement.[6]

Like "Death and Us," this essay refers obliquely to tensions between Jewish assimilationism and commitment to Jewish traditionalism. Unlike "Death and Us," however, this essay is intended for a non-Jewish audience. Any references to Jews, death, and the fantasy of immortality, central themes in the counterthesis we have traced through Freud's writings, remain well below the surface. The essay points toward, without addressing explicitly, an inquiry into the psychodynamics of the tension between assimilation and the rejection of assimilation.

References to the body of the mother lie below the surface of this text about land and the countryside as well. As Freud declared in *Introductory Lectures on Psychoanalysis,* "The complicated topography of the female genital parts makes one understand how it is that they are often represented as landscapes" (*SE* 15: 156). So the smiling countryside which becomes a devastated battlefield is, in some sense, the female body. We have traversed metaphoric landscapes with Freud before: the landscape of *The Interpretation of Dreams,* with its deep defiles, dark forests, and high vistas, was rather different from this landscape. *The Interpretation of Dreams* described a conquistador's journey, a heroic descent to the depths, and a triumphant discovery. "On Transience," on the other hand, describes a wiser and older traveler strolling through the once smiling, but now devastated countryside. If the journey in the dream book was in some sense a sexual exploration of the maternal body, the journey in "On Transience" is a journey traversing an aging maternal body toward death.[7] The symbolic landscapes Freud chooses to describe in his texts map a set of changing types of travel through diverse maternal terrains.

There is a deeper sense, as well, involving the metaphor of the "open wound," in which the topography of the maternal body underlies Freud's ideas about mourning and melancholia. Before turning to a discussion of that material, however, it will be useful to examine the work of a scholar who addresses a related theme, the significance of Freud's Jewish identity and his desire for assimilation in relation to mourning and "symbolic loss." This scholar is Peter Homans.

FREUD'S ABILITY TO MOURN AND THE ORIGINS OF PSYCHOANALYSIS

The theme of Jewish identity and its loss through assimilation to the dominant German cultural environment, I have argued, is a subtext of Freud's 1915 essays on mourning. Peter Homans brings these themes together in a different way. He draws upon Freud's analysis of mourning to develop a theory of the origins of psychoanalysis out of the loss of religion. Homans constructs a complex analysis of the introspective and individualistic orientation of contemporary Western culture as a product of the mourning of a lost sense of tradition and community.

Homans focuses not only on the broad symbolic losses of diminishing religious identity, but also on the personal symbolic losses in Freud's life. He specifically links Freud's publications of 1915 with the losses associated with Jung's departure from the psychoanalytic movement, Freud's interest in assimilation, and his related desire for the acceptance of psychoanalysis by a Gentile audience. He notes, for example, that symbolic loss was especially pronounced in Freud's life during four periods: the self-analysis following the death of his father in 1896, the break with Carl Jung in 1913, the period in the early and mid-1920s when his daughter Sophie and her son Heinerle died and when Freud himself was diagnosed with cancer, and the last few years of his life, when he wrote the "cultural texts" (1998: 80). Focusing in particular on the period following the break with Jung, Homans specifies that Freud's relationships with fellow Jews, especially Karl Abraham, "facilitated an ability to mourn the loss of Jung and especially of the realities

Jung stood for or symbolized." He goes on, "The ability to mourn affected Freud's self-definition (as did the earlier inability) and fostered fresh creativity. The yield was rich: 'On Narcissism,' 'The Moses of Michelangelo,' and (what else?) 'Mourning and Melancholia'" (80, parentheses in the original).

Homans's analysis of Freud as successful mourner of both individual, personal losses and the larger cultural losses of religious community deserves careful attention, for, in his view, it was precisely the loss and mourning of a Jewish background that created psychoanalysis. Homans uses an evocative metaphor to describe the relation of psychoanalysis to Judaism: psychoanalysis is to Judaism as a "key [is] to its wax impression" or a "statue to a plaster cast" (1989: 71). Homans's metaphor is widely embraced by those in Jewish cultural studies. Gilman, for example, introduces *Freud, Race, and Gender* by stating, "I endorse Peter Homans's model of Freud's response to the idea of 'Jewishness' as analogous to the relationship of 'a key to its wax impression' or a 'statue to a plaster cast of the statue' — psychoanalysis emerged as the negative image, so to speak, of its Jewish surroundings" (1993: 4; see also Boyarin 1994: 30 and Le Rider 1993: 294).

Homans's metaphor of wax impression or plaster cast is effective in part because of its polyvocality. The single image of "wax impression" holds multiple interpretive readings. It can be read as an argument for a positive influence of Judaism on Freud's life and work. From this perspective, psychoanalysis is, in some ways, a "Jewish science" in that it reflects Jewish traditions, methods, and ideas. The metaphor can also be read as an argument for a negative effect, rather than a positive effect. From this perspective, the wax or plaster may carry the impression of an ambivalence about Judaism, a secularized critique of Judaism, or a loss of Judaism. A third meaning is related to the above. The metaphor can be read as an argument for the effects of anti-Semitism. From this perspective, psychoanalysis was shaped in large part by the powerful ideologies hostile to Judaism.

Although all these meanings inform Homans's metaphor, the second meaning — the loss of Judaism due to secularization and assimilation — is dominant. His concern is with locating Freud's discovery of psychoanalysis within the context of the cultural shift toward rationalization described by Max Weber. Homans defines psychoanalysis as part of the modernization which affected a broad sweep of the West. Echoing his own metaphor, Homans describes his understanding of the origins of psychoanalysis as "fitt[ing] lock and key with Max Weber's account of value change in modern Western culture, which he described with the ideas of disenchantment and rationalization" (1989: 26).

From Homans's perspective, psychoanalysis is both a product of the mourning which accompanies modernization and a contributor to the losses which mark modernization. Psychoanalysis emerges out of the introspection and individuation which follow upon Freud's successful mourning of the loss of traditional Jewish communal and religious structures. At the same time, psychoanalysis introduces a systematic method which furthers the process of modernization by promoting introspection and individuation. Successfully deidealizing and mourning the loss of Jewish community and identity, Freud achieved an unprecedented level of introspective analytic access: he developed a remarkable ability to observe and recount the processes and contents of the unconscious. His theory of how the mind works was based on his introspective investigations of the unconscious initiated by the processes of loss and mourning.

Homans is not alone in lauding Freud's remarkable ability to observe and theorize the encounter with loss, death, and the process of mourning. While Homans finds Freud's psychoanalytic formulations emerging directly from his ability to mourn and his introspective probes into his own mourning psyche, Robert Jay Lifton similarly notes that Freud was "enormously sensitive to the idea of death" and suggests that his writings during the period of World War I were "an expression of a deepening of reflection on the part of a highly sensitive man faced with a new dimension of death saturation in his world" (in Caruth 1995: 129). And Jacques Le Rider argues that while a whole generation of Viennese modernists — Freud, Ludwig Wittgenstein, Theodor Herzl, Arthur Schnitzler, and others — lived through the experience of "the fading and loss of traditions" (1993: 294), Freud was the figure most capable of observing and theorizing the experience of that grief and loss.

Homans's analysis of the origins of psychoanalysis situates Freud's discovery within the historical and cultural changes marking the shift from premodernity to modernity. According to Homans, this detachment from common culture and this ability to mourn are not unique to Freud. He finds the pattern of loss of religious tradition followed by mourning and analytic access in several of Freud's predecessors and contemporaries, including not only his Jewish colleagues Karl Abraham and Otto Rank, but also such non-Jewish thinkers as Friederich Nietzsche, Max Weber, and Carl Jung. Homans shows that Freud's ideas about psyche and culture can be seen as part of a widespread set of "attempts to respond both critically and constructively — and not just reactively — to a sociohistorical sense of loss" (1989: 27). To put Homans's thesis into Freud's terminology, Freud successfully and without castration anxiety or misogynist panic encountered dangers to "Throne and Altar." It was Freud's ability to mourn the losses of these symbolic thrones and altars that gave rise to the creative ideas constituting psychoanalysis.

In a sense, Homans's thesis implies that all moderns are in mourning. Or, more precisely, it implies that all of us have experienced symbolic loss, which we may or may not be able to mourn successfully. Modernity, psychology, and individualism are products of the more or less successful mourning of the loss of common cultures and religious communities. The shift which gave rise to psychoanalysis can thus be seen as a microcosm of a much larger sociohistorical shift which continues to shape us today. We shall return to the broader implications of Homans's theory below, but first, let us turn to a discussion of one arena in which Freud seems to have been unable to mourn.[8]

MELANCHOLIA AND THE INABILITY
TO MOURN THE MOTHER

Freud was indeed a master mourner of both personal and social losses, particularly of religious losses, and a masterful observer of the process of mourning. But there are significant gaps and limitations in Freud's ability to mourn. Once again, these gaps cluster around the themes of the counterthesis. Let us contrast Freud's complex and insightful interpretations of the psychodynamics of loss in "Mourning and Melancholic" and in "On Transience" with his numb response to a set of losses described in other texts.

This theorist with a remarkable ability to mourn and to analyze his own mourning paradoxically felt "no grief" (*kein Trauer*) at his mother's death and could formulate no interpretation of the experience. In a letter of 1930 to Ernest Jones upon the death of his ninety-five-year-old mother, Freud wrote:

> I will not disguise the fact that my reaction to this event has, because of special circumstances, been a curious one. Assuredly, there is no saying what effects such an experience may produce in deeper layers, but on the surface I can detect only two things: an increase in personal freedom, since it was always a terrifying thought that she might come to hear of my death;[9] and secondly, the satisfaction that at last she has achieved the deliverance for which she had earned a right after such a long life. No grief otherwise, such as my ten years younger brother is painfully experiencing. I was not at the funeral; again Anna represented me. (Jones 1957: 162)[10]

He reiterated the phrase "no grief" in a letter to Ferenczi written a day later: "No pain, no grief, which is probably to be explained by the circumstances, the great age and the end of the pity we had felt at her helplessness" (Jones 1957: 162).

These statements of his lack of grief were, of course, in letters, not in metapsychological treatises. One might not expect analyses of the "effects in the deeper layers" in epistolary documents. But Freud's reiterated description of his reaction — "no grief" — may point toward something deeper. It resonates with a very similar remark in a famous footnote of another text. Describing the reaction to the death of *another* mother, the mother of the author of the game of disappearance and return, Freud stated, in a footnote mentioned earlier, "When this child was five-and-three-quarters, his mother died. Now that she was really 'gone' ('o-o-o'), the little boy showed no signs of grief" (*SE* 18: 16 n. 1). Although, as noted in chapter 2, Freud grieved deeply at his daughter's death, both Freud and the young child — his grandson Ernst — reacted to the deaths of their own mothers with "no grief."

Grief, *Trauer*, is the same word translated as "mourning" in "Mourning and Melancholia." By saying that he experienced no grief, Freud is saying that he did not mourn. We have seen that among the characteristics of melancholia are the refusal to mourn (a refusal of *Trauer*), and a demand for immortality. Is Freud's lack of *Trauer* at the death of his mother a sign that his reaction was melancholic, rather than mournful? Is this a demand for maternal immortality? A refusal to mourn? Freud's descriptions of melancholia in 1915, I suggest, provide an uncannily accurate portrayal of his own reaction many years later to his mother's death.[11]

Some theorists have found Freud's expression of *kein Trauer* problematic, pathological, and misogynist, indicative of problems in Freud's early relationship with his mother and symptomatic of problems in his theories of psyche and culture. In Madelon Sprengnether's interpretation of Freud's description of young Ernst's failure to experience grief at his mother's death, for example, the passage is a projection of Freud's own childhood experiences. She emphasizes the sentence which concludes Freud's famous footnote: "It is true that in the interval a second child had been born and had roused him to violent jealousy" (*SE* 18: 16 n. 1). Recalling Freud's account of his own childhood rage when a younger brother was born (Julius, who died in infancy), she draws the conclusion that in the account of Ernst's lack of grief, Freud deflects the infantile hostility he was unable to direct toward his own mother. He could admit freely a sense of hostility toward his younger brother, although he could not express anger toward his mother.[12] While Sprengnether finds parallels in the births of younger siblings, I find an even more striking parallel in Freud's attribution of "no signs of grief" to Ernst and Freud's expression of "no grief" at his own mother's death many years later, a parallel which may be an indication of a broader cultural pattern.

In an analysis that parallels Sprengnether's in its speculations on Freud's infancy and childhood, the psychoanalyst Ana Maria Rizzuto examines Freud's relationship with his mother, his decision not to attend her funeral, and his expression of "no grief" at her death in an attempt to explain Freud's atheism. She argues that Freud's lack of religious belief can be traced to a "profound disturbance in emotional attachment between mother and child" (1998: 235). She finds him unable to entrust himself to others and incapable of the "formation of an ego-syntonic God representation deserving belief" (235). While Freud's nurse or nanny did provide an important emotional bond, Rizzuto argues, the dismissal and departure of his nurse when he was less than three years old left him with a feeling of despair and led him to additional steps toward unbelief (265). In Rizzuto's view, his failure to grieve his mother's death, like his atheism, can be attributed primarily to his mother's early inability to be attentive to her son's emotional needs and to her lifelong narcissism (240).

Rizzuto's assumption that unbelief, agnosticism, and atheism are caused by failures in early emotional attachments and are accompanied by the inability to form lasting relationships is troubling, however. Troubling as well is the apparently unexamined assumption that faith and belief are normative, while unbelief is anomalous and pathological. Such a perspective provides little insight into the world of modernity, where, in many sectors of American and European society, unbelief is widespread, rather than anomalous, and where atheism or agnosticism correlate no more closely with dysfunctionality in relationships than do religious belief. Although I, too, argued in earlier chapters that the absence of God is often associated psychologically with fears and fantasies about maternal mortality and immortality (we found these concepts in "A Religious Experience," for example), Rizzuto's analysis is problematic in focusing entirely on the individual and the pathological. Her approach leaves little room for an understanding of the cultural changes accompanying modernity or for deeper analyses of widely shared unconscious fears and fantasies.

Contrary to Rizzuto, I suggest that Freud's response to his mother's death is far from idiosyncratic and pathological. Rather, it can be seen as an honest and insightful expression of his mental state and as an attempt to express the pattern of unconscious associations of mortality, maternity, and the demand for immortality that we have traced in this volume. Freud's words, "no grief," speak to a widespread problem: the inability to mourn the mother, a problem which inevitably emerges in the many experiences of separation from and temporary losses of the mother, in the many experiences of having been "slighted, neglected, or disappointed" that he describes as characteristics of melancholia (*SE* 14: 251). The difficulty in mourning the mother helps to explain the ubiquity (if not universality) of misogyny, both in the modern world and in other contexts.

As we have seen, Freud described two different reactions to loss within his texts on mourning from 1915. The first is a reaction that includes a refusal to mourn, an extended or incomplete process of mourning, and a conflicted demand for immortality. The second is a less conflicted reaction in which the loss is acknowledged, worked through, and resolved. In the first case, the case of melancholia, ambivalence toward the lost object extends and intensifies the process of mourning. At the same time, a demand for immortality results in an inability to allow mourning to follow its painful, but necessary course to resolution. In the second case, identified as mourning in both texts, the demand for immortality is abandoned and the mourner accepts transience, loss, grief, and pain. Mourning is about acknowledging mortality and transience. Melancholia, these texts suggest, is about the demand for immortality. This demand for immortality provides a hint that this paradigm involves the counterthesis we have been tracing, in which the theme of immortality is prominent.

Other hints that melancholia involves the counterthesis are evident in Freud's further remarks on the psychodynamics of melancholia. In melancholia, libido "flows out." His metaphors here echo his many references to the "castrated" female genitals. The "complex of melancholia," he states "behaves like an open wound, drawing to itself cathectic energies . . . emptying the ego until it is totally impoverished" (*SE* 14: 253). The metaphor of "open wound" was one he had used much earlier in a document sent to Fliess in 1895 outlining a preliminary theory of melancholia. Asking how the effects of melancholia can be explained, he speculated on an "internal hemorrhage" of libido, a libidinal "in-drawing which operates inhibitingly like a wound" with "excitation running out, as it were through a hole" (Masson 1985: 103–4; *SE* 1: 205–6). Freud's use of the terminology of an "open wound" and "hole" to describe melancholia is a subtle evocation of the dangerous, deadly, "castrated," and uncanny genitals of the uncanny mother we often have encountered in the counterthesis. Juliana Schiesari, too, reads Freud's use of the metaphor of "open wound" as a reference to the female genitals: "The very notion of an open wound already seems to evoke the question of castration and thus implicitly that of sexual difference" (1992: 41). Although Freud reiterates the image of the wound in the final paragraph of "Mourning and Melancholia" (*SE* 14: 258), he does not develop this formulation further in the text, turning aside, once again, from a more complete development of the components of the counterthesis.[13]

In the dominant formulation of the effects of mourning, on the other hand, Freud speculated that, having lost the object of its love and attachment, the unattached libido is withdrawn into the ego and an identification is formed in a process whereby internal psychic structures are created or built up as memorials to the lost object. In this process, identifications are established "with the abandoned object" through the growth of new psychic structures. Freud's rhetoric is poetic: "The shadow of the object fell upon the ego" (*SE* 14: 249). These identifications constructed out of shadows and absences lead to the growth of structures within the ego and to changes in personality. In this psychological process, Freud explains, "an object which was lost has been set up again inside the ego . . . an object cathexis has been replaced by an identification" (*SE* 19: 28). The resulting identifications and structures are the basis of what we know as character: "This kind of substitution has a great share in determining the form taken by the ego . . . it makes an essential contribution towards building up what is called its 'character'" (*SE* 19: 28–29). The ego, in other words, acts as a memorial or monument for the losses that created its structures: "The character of the ego is a precipitate of abandoned object-cathexes . . . it contains the history of those object choices" (*SE* 19: 29). We become, in this paradigm, what we have lost. The shadow of the lost object becomes the content of the ego.

In this formulation, then, psychological character emerges from loss as a kind of edifice erected upon absence. This description of the "building up" of character and the erection of identifications inscribes mourning with the imagery of phallic masculinity characterizing the Oedipal masterplot. Freud weaves the theory of mourning into the Oedipal theory. He even specifies that the earliest of the identifications built up upon loss are the identifications "derived from the dissolution of the Oedipus complex" (*SE* 14: 242).

Always inquisitive about origins and beginnings, Freud raised questions about the identities of the first of the lost loves which the ego inscribes, asking whom we internalize and memorialize in the earliest mournful or melancholic processes of creating a self. As one might expect with his attachment to the Oedipal masterplot, Freud finds the father positioned as the primary lost love object. Beneath the ego, he states, lies hidden the loss of the "first and most important identification, [the] identification with the father" (*SE* 19: 31).

The process by which mourning and melancholia occur, Freud says in "On Transience," is "a great riddle" (*SE* 14: 306), another of the great riddles he attempted to solve during his career. Many of his riddles had Oedipal solutions. But his explicit references to open wounds and the demand for immortality and his expressions of no grief, no mourning at the deaths of mothers suggest that the solution to the riddle of melancholia is not entirely Oedipal.

In spite of Freud's insistence regarding the centrality of the loss of the father, other theorists of psychoanalysis have identified the prototypical lost object in mourning and ego formation as the mother. Madelon Sprengnether writes (and here I agree with Sprengnether) that "the body of the mother would seem to signal the process of mourning" (1990: 230). She goes on to suggest that the ego "owes its existence to an originary loss [of the mother], its very structure predicated on an absence" (1990: 228). In Sprengnether's reading, then, the loss that first creates the ego is the loss of the mother. The ego internalizes an absence, a state of incompleteness, deriving from the separation from the body of the mother. Other theorists concur, arguing that the mother is the original lost object and that "all subsequent experiences of loss . . . will be reminiscent of the loss of his mother" (Capps 1997: 15; cf. Jones 1996, 3–4).

Freud suggested that the ego is a fragile construction made of shadows of lost objects. Others state that the lost object is, in the first instance, the mother or the mother's body. Perhaps then we can say that the ego or self is constructed of a mix of melancholic open wounds that cannot heal and of the products of mourning: psychic structures that enact memorials or scars grown over the first and later losses and separations. Sprengnether believes that most of us successfully mourn the mother, although, in her view — shared by Rizzuto, Estelle Roith, and others — Freud did not.

In my view, however, none of us can fully mourn the mother. To mourn the mother would be to identify with her, to become her. And we cannot identify with or become the mother because, as D. W.

Winnicott (1972) and Julia Kristeva (1982) show, the separation from her is necessary for the birth and continuity of the self. A union with her would symbolize fragmentation, death, and annihilation. The clinical literature suggests it would lead to schizophrenic disintegration (Grunberger 1988, Rheingold 1967).

Freud's inability to grieve or mourn the mother expressed in his statement of no grief at his mother's death is, then, an inability we all share. The melancholic response to the separation from the mother is part of what gives rise to the self. If that mourning is always partly melancholic or troubled, then we are all melancholic mourners of lost mothers. In the variations and vicissitudes of mourning and melancholia, we encounter the familiar signals of the uncanny: maternity, mortality, and the demand for immortality. Death, absence, and loss are the precipitating events of mourning and melancholia. The strange, yet familiar body of the mother is the corpus or corpse or "open wound" underlying both. And the "demand for immortality" and the "refusal to mourn" obstructs the mourning process wherein losses are paradoxically "immortalized" in psychological structures.

Melancholia and the uncanny seem to be closely related. Donald Capps suggests that "the lost object identified in 'Mourning and Melancholia' is the mother who has become *unheimlich,* the one who arouses anxiety" (1997: 20). The loss of the mother that gives rise to the self involves, thus, not only a loss of a beloved, benign, nurturant, or as Winnicott says, "good enough" mother. A darker, more dangerous mother, an uncanny mother, or a mother who must be abjected will also be both present and absent, found and lost.

This chapter began with a discussion of Freud's analysis of the emergence of misogynist panic and anxiety in times of crisis and transition, times of dangers to "Throne and Altar." With this simple image Freud offered a condensed theory of the crisis of modernity and the near inevitability of misogyny in modernity. As we have seen, Freud mourned the losses of thrones and altars, observing how mourning occurs and developing theories about the process, rather than falling into panic.

Freud mapped the territory of mourning, producing the method and theory of psychoanalysis through careful attention to his own sense of loss and through careful observation of his own reactions to the dangers of "Throne and Altar." This chapter has shown, however, that Freud is only partially successful at mourning losses, symbolic and real. He was a better mourner of Jewish identities in transition than of maternal losses. His reaction to his mother's death is melancholic, rather than mournful.

Freud's inability to mourn the mother and his inability to theorize the mother of the counterthesis fully was not misogynist, idiosyncratic, or pathological. His tentative articulation of the counterthesis and his inability to pursue it further were symptomatic of a broad cultural pattern in which fantasies of immortality are intertwined with ideas about maternity, death, and the uncanny. It is not just the case that, in the words of Harold Bloom, "Freud's peculiar strength was to say what could not be said, or at least to attempt to say it, thus refusing to be silent in the face of the unsayable" (1995: 113). The counterthesis involved not just the unsayable, but the unspeakable.

Guessing at
What Lies Beneath

Much of what we do as scholars involves creating or selecting patterns within texts and fashioning those patterns into coherent narratives about the texts. We develop meaningful narratives out of other narratives in a process involving creation and discovery at the same time. Freud's major creation and discovery was the Oedipal theory with which he constructed a coherent narrative out of the "texts" of his own life and the lives of his patients, a narrative which informed the corpus of texts that make up his writings. Our creation and discovery has been another narrative, a shadowy but meaningful one, within Freud's texts. We have attended carefully to elements that fall outside the Oedipal framework, elements that have no place in a coherent Oedipal saga. To borrow Freud's words, "We have treated as Holy Writ what previous writers have regarded as arbitrary improvisation" (*SE* 5: 514). We have constructed a narrative in which the peripheral becomes central. This other narrative is what I have called a counterthesis.

Freud's Oedipal narrative, as we know well, tells a story of father-son tension and mother-son love. It attempts to understand and explain cultural patterns of resistance and submission to authoritarian figures and structures. Its central themes are desire and renunciation, rebellion and obedience. What can finally be said about the counterthesis we have illuminated in Freud's texts? What kind of narrative have we uncovered? What does it explain?

Although this narrative is shadowy and fragmentary, it is not completely obscure. It tells a story of fears and fantasies involving maternal loss, dead, deadly, uncanny mothers, and immortality. It explores anxieties about Jewishness, circumcision, castration, and assimilation. It examines our mournful and melancholic encounters with personal loss and social change. It attempts to explain the sources of misogyny and xenophobia in psyche and culture. It endeavors to "speak the unspeakable."

THE COUNTERTHESIS IN
CONTEMPORARY CULTURE

I have argued that the fears and fantasies explored in the counterthesis are not unique to Freud's personal psychology, but are widespread in our culture. If my speculations are correct, we should see evidence of these fears and fantasies today. What forms do they take in contemporary culture and what sorts of effects do they produce?

Seeking contemporary examples of these uncanny themes, I turned to the "virtual" world of the Internet. A short search brought me to the home page of the web site IHateWomen.com. Flaming, vibrating letters on a black background spell out "I Hate Women." The dominant graphic is an image of — who else? — Sigmund Freud. He stands, posed authoritatively over his famous words, "The great question which I have not been able to answer despite my thirty years of research into the feminine soul is 'What does a woman want?'" Displayed above a pair of thorny roses dripping with chillingly realistic blood, a multicolored text reads, "Valentine's Day is almost here. Do you have a pile of dog crap ready for the women you hate? Or perhaps showing your love with a bouquet of dead flowers would be more appropriate. . . . Visit dead-roses.com to find the perfect gift."

Links are offered to GetRevenge.com, SlapDaBitches.com, and

WomenSuck.org. A hyperlink takes me to "Thee Holy Woman Document," where misogynist aphorisms attributed to Freud, Jung, Nietzsche, and others are listed. Among them are the following:

No woman loves her child.
If the female role changes then men begin to lose their identity.
In love you have two people's hell to contend with.
A wise man seeks life, but woman is suicide.

The site requires little commentary. It illustrates vividly many of the themes we have encountered in a very different register in our discussion of Freud's counterthesis. Misogyny, matriphobia, death, and the abject are clearly visible. There are allusions to the absence of God in the ironically titled "Thee Holy Woman Document." Perhaps the most uncanny element in this web site is the Valentine's Day message, with its bloody imagery and its suggested "gifts" of excrement and dead flowers. As if to reverse the direction of the "unspeakable" effects of the uncanny mother, excrement, blood, and death are presented to the woman by the man: horror and abjection are his gift to her.

What are the effects of such fantasies? The site communicates a veiled threat of violence. One passage in "Thee Holy Woman Document" asks, "What is worse: the physical violence of a man or the emotional violence of women?" The text concludes, "A woman's imagination is much more dark and vicious." And the link to SlapDaBitches.com promises, "It's fun!" The IHateWomen.com web site clearly promotes a worldview hostile to women, connecting its visitors to a group of similar web sites created by and for like-minded readers and legitimating violence. Yet it has no direct institutional manifestation. It exists in an electronic underworld connected only indirectly to social practices.

Other sites touting similar ideas, however, represent web-based versions of real-world political institutions and social practices. Anti-abortion web sites, like the home page for Operation Rescue West (operationrescue.org), use images of horror and disgust to communicate their messages. Photos of mangled, bloody fetuses and jars of waste are visibly displayed. The theme of the uncanny mother is evoked in both text and image: the pregnant woman seeking an abortion is, in the imagery of the web site, a deadly mother, dangerous to her fetus. A matricidal rage against pro-choice women is expressed in photographs and stories about babies "saved" from their murderous mothers by abortion-clinic demonstrators. The theme of immortality is prominent in these sites: salvation and eternal life through Jesus is promised. A fetus begs, "Won't you tell my mommy about Jesus?"[1] And an image of the infant Jesus is inscribed with the words, "Think about it. Our Lord Jesus Christ came from heaven to earth to save us from our sins." The conflict between the presence and absence of God is displayed in colorful headlines: "Abortionist attacks Christians!" Even the theme of anti-Semitism appears, albeit in disguised and projected form. Headlines define abortion clinics as the true "death camps": "American Holocaust: See inside a Death Camp." The imagery of the counterthesis is vividly evident.

The threat of violence is ubiquitous, but displaced. Violence, the rhetoric of the site suggests, comes from women seeking to end pregnancies, from pro-choice protesters, or from doctors who perform abortions. A running tally of "babies murdered by abortion" increases by the second, and a story of a woman's death from a "botched abortion" fills a sidebar. But the history of violence against women perpetrated by anti-abortion protesters at clinics and hospitals is a disturbing testimony to the actual source of the violence and to the real world effects of these fears and fantasies.

The Internet is full of sites like these. I need not detail the neo-Nazi, anti-Semitic web sites and the tragic practices they encourage. Do these web sites "speak the unspeakable"? No: they express it. They manipulate it without awareness. In Freud's terminology, they "repeat" it or "act it out." In a description of the unconscious reenactment of the repressed or forgotten, Freud explains, the patient "does not remember anything of what he has forgotten and repressed, but acts it out. He reproduces it not as a memory but as an action; he repeats it, without, of course, knowing that he is repeating it . . . the greater the resistance, the more extensively will acting out (repetition) replace remembering" (*SE* 12: 150–51). The "acting out" on these web sites is a repetition without understanding of the fears and fantasies of the counterthesis.

I have suggested that healing and transformation result from the ability to understand and claim as our own the uncanny material of Freud's counterthesis. But understanding is only part of what makes transformation possible in Freud's "talking cure." Freud explains the gradual process of healing in the context of the therapeutic relationship: insight, awareness, and understanding or "remembering" are followed by a slow and patient "working through" of resistance. One must allow the patient time "to work through it [the resistance], to overcome it by continuing . . . the analytic work." The working through of resistance, he adds, "may in practice turn out to be an arduous task" (*SE* 12: 155). He reiterates elsewhere that "real changes in ourselves take place slowly; if they occur rapidly, suddenly, that is a bad sign" (*SE* 22: 156).

In the context of the "talking cure," the element that makes possible the remembering and the working through is the transference, the relationship of patient to therapist: "The main instrument . . . for curbing the patient's compulsion to repeat and for turning it into a motive for remembering lies in the handling of the transference" (*SE* 12: 154). But psychoanalysis for an entire culture is impossible. How, in the cultural arena, might we move from "acting out" to understanding without access to the transference relationship between therapist and patient? While there is no exact parallel to the transference in the cultural arena, Freud's description of the transference points toward a functional equivalent. The transference, he explains, "creates an intermediate region between illness and real life through which the transition from the one to the other is made. . . . From the repetitive reactions which are exhibited in the transference we are led along the familiar paths to the awakening of memories" (*SE* 12: 154).

Drawing on D. W. Winnicott's notion of "transitional space," I sug-

gest that the realms of art, literature, and religion often serve as a kind
of transferential, transitional, or intermediate region (Winnicott 1972).
The intermediate space of the transference finds an effective cultural
parallel in film, for example. In its ability to integrate word and image,
in the communal space of the theater, and in its narratives bridging illusion and reality, film creates a transitional or "intermediate region" similar to the transference. Some films merely "act out" unconscious fears
and fantasies, but others provide the space in which the imagery of the
counterthesis, under certain conditions, might be transformed, remembered, and worked through.

Alfred Hitchcock's *Vertigo,* produced in 1958, remains relevant today
as an attempt to "speak the unspeakable." *Vertigo* involves a fantasy of
the reincarnation or immortality of three women who are in fact one
woman. The uncanny "revenant" is desired, dead, and deadly. Hitchcock creates a narrative full of repetitions and returns that invite
reflection: true and false suicides, murders disguised as suicides, and
accidental deaths are intertwined. The story is carried forward by identities destroyed and re-created in an intellectually complex and aesthet-
ically stunning narrative of a man's obsessive encounter with love and
death. Hitchcock's film encourages thought, analysis, and understanding. Unlike the misogynist discourse of IHateWomen.com or the shrill
rhetoric of the Operation Rescue web site, both of which admittedly
draw upon some of the same emotions and images as *Vertigo,* Hitchcock's film initiates a mournful meditation on death, loss, and love. By
no means does it encourage violence.[2] Thus, like the psychoanalytic
transference, film serves as a transitional realm within which we are
offered opportunities to remember and work through our own stories
of uncanny mothers.

Learning to speak the unspeakable, whether through psychoanalysis or through reflection on cultural phenomena like film, may, in the
cultural arena, lead to new possibilities for understanding between
groups currently divided by seemingly unbridgeable gaps. Let us
return to the rhetoric of the abortion debate for an example of such a

possibility. The pro-choice community dismisses the rhetoric of pro-life groups, preferring to see abortion as a rational choice by a woman about her own body and her own future without loss, mourning, or other serious consequences (see, for example, prochoice.about.com). This discourse avoids the emotionally charged imagery of life and death, blood and bodily fluids, loss and grief, immortality, matripho-bia, and matricide. The rhetoric of the pro-life community, on the other hand, "acts out" the uncanny themes of the counterthesis. While their "acting out" and their conclusions are problematic, they are, in fact, correct that the decision to abort a pregnancy brings us face to face with the confluence of maternity, mortality, and immortality, with life and death in the womb, with that "uncanny home" that is simultane-ously womb and tomb.

If the pro-life and pro-choice communities could both acknowledge that abortion inevitably brings about an encounter with our fears and fantasies about uncanny and dangerous mothers *and* that it is some-times a choice that must be made, then perhaps steps toward reconcili-ation would be possible. If we could, in other words, acknowledge the "unspeakable" that underlies the issue of abortion, yet, at the same time, acknowledge the necessity of occasional "unspeakable" acts, then per-haps these seemingly irreconcilable groups could move away from vio-lent encounters. Freud's counterthesis, and films like Hitchcock's *Vertigo,* initiate a "speaking of the unspeakable" with full understand-ing that we all share these fears and fantasies. Our ability to speak of these ideas with insight and ownership may begin to free us from entrapment in their virulent networks of reenactment.

IMPLICATIONS FOR THE STUDY OF RELIGION

What are the implications of this analysis of Freud's counterthesis for the study of religion in modernity? In the context of the secularizing forces and rapid changes marking modernity, all religions are in transition.

We continually encounter new losses of traditional religious forms, new religious pluralisms, and new forms of secularism. Freud's theory emerged from the cultural shifts of the late nineteenth and early twentieth centuries, yet his ideas will continue to serve us well in a twenty-first-century world marked by loss, change, and ongoing instability. The study of religion in modernity must involve the study of the absence of religion, as well as its presence, the study of change and transition in religion and of how we mourn those losses, changes, and transitions.

I have argued that Freud's writings reveal a gendered deep structure undergirding both religion and its loss. The *Heimlichkeit* of Jewishness, I suggested, was closely associated with the *unheimlich,* uncanny mother, while the *Unheimlichkeit* of circumcision served as a disguise for the abjection associated with the maternal body. The gendering of religion is particularly visible in the fin de siècle renegotiations of masculinity, femininity, and Jewishness characterizing Freud's Vienna, but it is likely to be relevant to religion and its transformations in contemporary forms, as well.

Our inquiry into the theme of immortality provides an important example of the unconscious gendering of religion. As we saw in chapter 2, in a rationalist, Enlightenment-based argument, Freud urged the renunciation of the idea of the afterlife, insisting that it not only serves as an infantile wish fulfillment, but also obstructs social progress. His counterthesis suggests, however, that belief in the afterlife is not easily abandoned, for it is deeply intertwined with fantasies of maternity and mortality. If religious ideas today are often communicated in movie theaters rather than churches, and if Hitchcock's *Vertigo* provides a hint of how we envision immortality in modernity, immortality is clearly associated with the uncanny female body. We cannot ignore the question of whether and how uncanny mothers, sexuality, and death are intertwined at the deeper levels with these new formulations of immortality. As we study gender, religion, and the loss of religion in modernity, we will continue to find Freud a useful guide.

TELLING SECRETS

Finally, therefore, let us return to Freud in order to ask why he was unable to explore the content of the counterthesis more directly. Why are his inquiries into the counterthesis so hesitant, fragmented, or deferred? Oedipal secrets involving fantasies about the death of the father were discovered by the forty-year-old Freud after his father died in 1896. Secrets involving fantasies about the death of the mother, however, remained virtually untold. "Freud has the style," Philip Rieff notes, "to keep many a little secret from himself . . . rarely, for example, did Freud probe his relationship to his mother" (Rieff 1979: 391). This reticence to know or tell the secrets, as we saw earlier, can be explained, in part, by the powerful sense of the truth of the Oedipal theory and by Freud's personal identification with the Oedipal saga. Freud's reticence can also be attributed in part to the fact that his mother lived until 1930, dying at age ninety-five, when Freud was seventy-three. But her actual longevity is only part of the paradigm that makes her psychologically immortal. We all need our mothers to be immortal, for, like Freud, who felt *kein Trauer,* no grief, we cannot mourn our mothers.

David Bakan, who has considered carefully the psychodynamics of telling secrets about oneself, indicates that one may "reveal a fabricated 'secret,' or a less-secret secret" in order to conceal a more significant secret and to "generate the impression that one is being open and frank" (1967: 195).[3] Freud reveals the Oedipal secrets (the less-secret secrets) in order to conceal the deeper secrets of the counterthesis, which could be spoken only in veiled or hesitant speech. The secret *(Geheimnis)* of one's original home *(Heim)* remains too uncanny *(Unheimlich)* — and too closely associated with death — to be openly recounted. Speaking the unspeakable is no easy task.

In "The Theme of the Three Caskets," Freud articulates the riddle of death, the mother, and the uncanny: "The fairest and best of women who has taken the place of the Death-Goddess has kept certain characteristics that border on the uncanny. . . . From them we have been able to guess at what lies beneath" (SE 12: 300). Freud's incompletely articulated counterthesis offers a promising and provocative reading of misogyny and xenophobia and hints at the vivid presence of something lying beneath. Had Freud been able to pursue the counterthesis more directly, he might have pointed clearly toward the psychodynamics of this melancholic pattern in which we persist in associating the mother with death, the uncanny, immortality and the afterlife, the absence of God, and the Jew. But his hesitant efforts to speak the unspeakable allow us nevertheless to "guess at what lies beneath."

NOTES

INTRODUCTION

1. The counterthesis is related, however, to subsequent developments in the work of Winnicott and Klein.

2. Madelon Sprengnether's complex and wide-ranging book *The Spectral Mother* begins as a feminist "critique" of psychoanalysis, proceeds to develop an "inclusive" perspective, and concludes on an "analytic" note. The volume spans my three categories.

3. Arguably, one can find in Freud's texts a tendency to essentialize "the woman" and to conflate the feminine with the maternal. I read many of these formulations, however, as efforts at the analysis of such essentialisms and conflations.

4. Foucault's interest was in the emergent "science of sexuality," the discursive production of power, and the propagation of knowledge constituting a science of sexuality. He critiqued the idea of the "repressive hypothesis," the notion that the relationship between sex and culture is a simple, one-dimensional process of cultural repression. He challenged in particular the Romantic notion that sex was once repressed and taboo, that Freud simply lifted the repression, and that we are now, or soon will be, sexually liberated.

5. Stephen Friedlander emphasizes that in the psychoanalytic view, culture

"constrains individual behavior . . . to the extent that the individual becomes embedded in the system of signification that originates in the outer world. The unconscious constrains the individual subject compelling him/her to function according to a system of obligations which reflects their unconscious interpretation" of their situation (1996: 172). Friedlander's words are meant to describe Lacan's view of the intersections of culture and the unconscious in contrast to Freud's. Lacan, however, usually situates his own reading of culture and the unconscious in congruity with Freud's. In my view, Friedlander's description fits Freud's approach as well as it fits Lacan's.

6. Chanter's own answer to this important question is that positioning oneself in relation to a "master discourse" (her focus is on Irigaray's rereading of Levinas) is, in fact, a risk worth taking.

7. See Rand and Torok (1997) for another analysis of contradictory theories of mental functioning in Freud's work. See Gilligan (1984) for a discussion of contradictions in Freud's work regarding the psychology of women. See Freud (*SE* 14: 201) for the differentiation of the "word presentation" *(Wortvorstellung)* from the "thing presentation" *(Dingvorstellung).*

8. Freud describes the "mystic writing pad" as a "small contrivance that . . . can in fact provide both an ever ready receptive surface and permanent traces of the notes that have been made upon it" (*SE* 19: 228). He draws an analogy to the human mind: "If we imagine one hand writing upon the surface of the mystic writing pad while another periodically raises its covering sheet from the wax slab, we shall have a concrete representation of the . . . functioning of the perceptual apparatus of our mind" (*SE* 19: 232). I extend Freud's metaphor to the complex layering of masterplot and counterthesis.

9. Boyarin argues that Freud's abandonment of the seduction theory and adoption of the Oedipal theory must be understood within the historical context of European ideologies of gender and race in the 1890s. He shows that an alternative masculinity obtained within Judaism, in opposition to and in critique of the "muscular masculinity" which constituted the "dominant fiction." The alternative male was a gentle, nurturing scholar for whom feminization was experienced as neither a threat nor a danger (1997: xvii). Boyarin suggests that Freud's discovery of the Oedipus complex can be seen as a response to a major cultural shift: as the feminized Jewish male became a dangerous identity, Freud discovered a way to affirm a masculine, heterosexist developmental model in which boys' desires are for mothers and hostility is directed toward fathers. Thus, in Boyarin's view, Freud's discovery of the Oedipus complex

"was not . . . a product of his own private psychological development, but part of a larger sociohistorical history" produced by a nexus of historical forces that included the pathologizing of the homosexual, and the racialization of the Jews and the gendering of anti-Semitism (1997: 220).

CHAPTER 1

1. Virgil, *Aeneid* 7.312. Freud leaves the passage in Latin. This translation, in the footnote to Freud's text, is provided by Strachey.

2. Virgil's words have a complex history in Freud's intellectual trajectory and a complex history of interpretation in the literature on psychoanalysis. As early as 1896, Freud had announced to Fliess his plan to use the line as a motto for introducing a different text, an essay on symptom formation: "The psychology of hysteria will be preceded by the proud words *'Introite et hic dii sunt'* . . . the symptom formation by *'Flectere si nequeo superos Acheronta movebo'"* (Masson 1985: 205). (The "Introite" passage ["Enter, for the gods dwell here as well"], a quote from Aristotle's "De Partibus Animalium" 1.5, was a popular one among the early psychoanalysts. Carl Jung carved it on the lintel above his front door.) Three years later, Freud mentioned Virgil's words specifically as his motto for *The Interpretation of Dreams,* where he stated that it was not his first choice. Fliess had nixed an unidentified passage from Goethe that he had earlier selected (Masson 1985: 361). In addition, he used it in 1909 in one of his lectures at Clark University (Editor's note, *SE:* 5: 608). Bakan provocatively interprets the "flectere" passage as a reference to the tension between God (the superego) and the Devil (the suspended superego) in a "satanic pact" in which permission is granted to "violate the precepts of the superego," making it possible for the "suppressed material to rise to consciousness" (Bakan 1958: 210–11). Thanks are due to Don Capps for reminding me of this passage in Bakan's book.

In the same 1896 letter in which he first staked claim on Virgil's words, Freud also stated, reporting on a recent period of depression, "My bad time has run its course. . . . [I] am not in the least interested in life after death" (Masson 1985: 204–5). In a previous letter, he had described his period of depression: "what I am lacking completely are high spirits and pleasure in living; instead, I am busy noting the occasions when I have to occupy myself with the state of affairs after my death." Masson responds to these remarks with a brief footnote: "Meaning unclear" (Masson 1985: 204). But Rizzuto finds much to say about this material. She finds evidence of "religious thinking modulated by negation, displacement and sublimation." She finds Freud defensive and disingenuous in denying an interest in life after death, and she argues that "he could not stop the return to consciousness of derivatives of unconscious God representations. His preoccupation with God and the underworld appeared in displaced, and sublimated form" in the reference to Virgil's words (Rizzuto 1998: 254). I read these remarks of Freud's somewhat differently. I see them as evidence that in 1896, shortly after the death of his father, even as he was formulating the Oedipus complex, he was also formulating an alternate view: the counterthesis.

3. Freud provides hints about the gendered meaning of the landscape in *Introductory Lectures on Psychoanalysis,* noting that pubic hair "is depicted in dreams as woods and bushes." He adds, "the complicated topography of the female genital parts makes one understand how it is that they are often represented as landscapes, with rocks, woods, and water" (*SE* 15: 156). Hyman reiterates Freud's gender analysis: "All of these dark woods, narrow defiles, high grounds, and deep penetrations are unconscious sexual imagery and we are exploring a woman's body — that of Freud's mother" (Hyman 1962: 333; cf. Shengold 1991: 50). Yet, as we shall see, this is not simply an Oedipal fantasy.

4. He was reading Dante at this time (Jones 1953: 380). I find parallels as well to Augustine's *Confessions.* Like Augustine's masterpiece, Freud's dream book is unquestionably an introspective confession of personal sins and desires, artfully arrayed with the intent of bringing the reader closer and closer to the "truth."

5. See Shengold, who notes that both Freud's and Dante's masterpieces were composed by men in their early forties writing of their younger selves. Both works describe a pilgrimage toward knowledge, and both works recount journeys of the soul (1991: 47–48).

6. Weiner notes: "Wagner never included the word *Jude* in his words for the stage because he didn't need to; the corporeal features deemed obvious signs of the Jew in his culture would have made the antisemitic nature of his representations of purportedly Jewish characteristics self-evident in his time" (13).

7. Might these subversions of the royal road be evident as well in hints and hesitations Freud provides about the geography of the journey itself? His hesitation is evident in this passage from the beginning of chapter 7 of *The*

Interpretation of Dreams: "Before starting off along this new path, it will be well to pause and look around, to see whether, in the course of our journey we have overlooked anything of importance . . . the easy and agreeable portion of our journey lies behind us. Hitherto, unless I am greatly mistaken, all the paths along which we have traveled have led us to the light — toward elucidation and fuller understanding. But as soon as we endeavor to penetrate more deeply into the mental process involved in dreaming, every path will end in darkness . . . we must be careful (*SE* 5: 511). Freud's references to "uncertainties" and "incompleteness" and his concern that "every path will end in darkness" may be reflections of anxieties about the counterthesis. See James DiCenso (1999) for an analysis of other examples of Freud's complex and liberating strategies for deconstructing some of his own more rigid theses.

8. Derrida notes that it is difficult to decide whether "'one must' . . . records an unsurpassable limit . . . or whether it is a 'one must' of duty that institutes what one *must* do, which is not to go beyond, or if you prefer, what one *must not* do, which is to go beyond, because that has no meaning" (Derrida 1998: 14). The "unsurpassable limit" seems the most likely choice to me. Capps (personal communication) opts for the "'one must' of duty."

9. Freud identified weaving as women's invention, developed to cover the genitals out of shame over the absence of the phallus (*SE* 22: 132).

10. "What forever exceeds the analysis of the dream is indeed a knot that cannot be untied, a thread that, even if it is cut, like an umbilical cord, nevertheless remains forever knotted, right on the body, at the place of the navel. This scar is a knot against which analysis can do nothing" (Derrida 1998: 11).

11. Kofman, too, sees a connection between *The Interpretation of Dreams* and "Medusa's Head": "the intimate, shameful secrets that Freud fears to expose to the public, because of the horror they are very likely to arouse, are thus inseparably linked with his Jewishness and with femininity, with castration anxiety. In this sense *The Interpretation of Dreams* is another "Medusa's Head" (1985: 32).

12. Some theorists addressing this turning aside at the "navel of the dream" find fault with Freud for this gesture. Kofman, for example, argues that while Oedipus solved the riddle of the feminine, Freud could not. "Only the man who has no fear of the incest transgression can go looking for it there. Oedipus alone was able to answer the riddle of the Sphinx, the enigma of femininity, by going to steal from the very womb of Mother Nature her most inviolable secrets" (1985: 94). In turning aside at this point, Kofman insists, Freud aban-

dons the psychoanalytic project: he "gives way before the mother, who alone holds the secret, the solution to the riddle" (1985: 94). Elements of Kofman's reading are correct: Freud *did* turn aside at the "navel of the dream," and the navel *is* a reference to the mother's body. Yet this turning aside is an important site for interpretation, rather than a reason to reject Freud: the gesture is an indication that Freud saw the limitations of his dominant narrative paradigm.

13. An anonymous reader for the University of California Press objects that Freud's language here is not about the "absence of God," but about rebellion against or submission to a very present God (psychical father of childhood). The reader argues that the American doctor's concern is existence or nonexistence of God, while Freud's concern is the attitude toward a God who exists psychically. This is an important issue, but my sense is that this reader is attending to the explicit text, while I am attending to a subtext. The doctor's temporary disbelief makes God absent. Freud's own atheism constructs a similarly absent or nonexistent God. Freud's explicit interpretation traces the shift from rebellion against a father who requires submission. A subtext traces a shift from a dead mother and an absent God to a living and loving mother and a present God. I thank the anonymous reader, however, for the thoughtful critique.

14. For other indications of Freud's sense of the "truth" of psychoanalysis, see *SE* 21: 36: "Psychoanalysis is a method of research, an impartial instrument, like the infinitesimal calculus." For the "immortality" of psychoanalysis, see *SE* 5: 453.

15. "Humor," according to Strachey, was written in the second week of August, 1927; "A Religious Experience" was written at the end of the same year (*SE* 21: 160; 168).

16. "Among the customs by which the Jews made themselves separate, that of circumcision has made a disagreeable, uncanny impression" (*SE* 23: 91).

17. Rizzuto corrects Freud's memory, dating this dream as October 3, 1865, when Freud was nine and a half years old (1998: 216). See also Rand and Torok (1997).

18. See Rheingold (1967: 97) for a discussion of the clinical literature on the death wish for the mother.

19. See Geller (1993).

20. See Bronfen (1992).

21. Rizzuto (1998) links Freud's collection of antiquities (Egyptian, Greek, Roman, etc.) to his memories of reading the Philippson Bible with his father

and to his grief over his father's death. The collection was a "god representation" of sorts for him, although, in her view, a weak and inadequate one. See chapter 5 for a further discussion of Rizzuto's thesis.

22. See also Robert Jay Lifton's remarks in an interview with Cathy Caruth: Freud "was enormously sensitive to the idea of death; but he too felt it necessary to leave death out conceptually. So that the only place you really find death, conceptually, in Freud, is in the death instinct, which tells us about Freud's awareness of the pervasive influence of death, or some representation of death for us psychologically." Lifton goes on to argue that Freud "sexualized the death experience" (in Caruth 1995: 129).

CHAPTER 2

1. Klein (1975), Beers (1992), Sprengnether (1990), Rizzuto (1998), and Brown (1959) do examine fantasies associating death and the mother; Homans (1989: 98) links Freud's attitude toward his own mother with fantasies of mortality and immortality. But none of these theorists have noted the more complex connections among these ideas.

2. See Freud's essay "On Negation," in which he argues that negation or denial represent proof of repression and therefore proof of the psychic reality of an idea. Here, apparently, a denial is just a denial, to paraphrase Freud's famous line about cigars.

3. Freud's theory of the death instinct may have emerged from his perceptions of cancerous cell growth within his own body: David Bakan suggests that Freud's attunement to the unconscious allowed him to perceive the most subtle physiological and endopsychic processes at the cellular level (1966: 156–78). Freud's speculations on cellular death wishes and cellular forms of deathlessness *(Unsterblichkeit)* are not far from current findings in microbiology. Clark (1996) discusses the theory of a cellular suicide gene, while Gold (1985) describes the deactivation of the "death gene" in the apparently deathless "HeLa" cells.

4. Here, Freud links misogyny with homosexuality. Elsewhere, Boyarin (1997) points out, Freud associates misogyny with homophobia.

5. This is not Freud's only reference to these words. They appear as well in a letter to Fliess in 1899 (Masson 1985: 343), in "Thoughts for the Times on War and Death," and in "Death and Us," a lecture presented to the B'nai B'rith

in 1915: "Everyone owes Nature a death and must expect to pay the debt" (*SE* 14: 289; cf. Freud, 1993: 12). These passages are discussed further in chapter 3.

6. See Anzieu and Rohde-Dachser for different interpretations of this passage. According to Anzieu, the displacement is not an indication of atheism, but of a "disturbing mother figure" (1986: 365). Rohde-Dachser, a feminist critic, argues that Freud's personal experience of the mother is of subordinate importance. More significant, she suggests, are the connections between nature, mother, and death in Freud's theory of culture (1991: 133).

7. As we saw in chapter 1, in Freud's "specimen dream" of Irma's injection in *The Interpretation of Dreams,* he noted his associations to a dream image of "three women": his wife, the nearly dead Irma, and Irma's friend. This dream of one woman who is actually three women was the context for Freud's first reference to the "navel of the dream" where interpretation ceases. Freud hinted at the dangerous nature of the triple woman or triple goddess in a letter to Fliess written shortly after finishing *The Interpretation of Dreams,* just as he was beginning his next project: "I would have liked to write to you about the sexual theory . . . it is only that I do not yet have the slightest idea what to do with the + + + female aspect, and that makes me distrust the whole thing" (Masson 1985: 382). Masson explains in a footnote: "Freud draws three crosses. This sign was sometimes chalked on the inside of doors in peasant houses to protect against danger" (382). Three crosses, three women: Freud seems to encounter dangerous, deadly women at every turn. His (partial) solution to this danger lies in his attempt to analyze it.

8. When Freud was given an ancient Grecian vase by Marie Bonaparte, he thanked her by saying, "It's a pity one can't take it to the grave" (Jones 1957: 169). Ironically, Bonaparte's gift did become, in a sense, Freud's casket. His ashes were put in the vase after his death.

9. See Rohde-Dachser (1991: 134), who notes Freud's persistent association of nature, death or Thanatos, and the mother. Sprengnether notes these connections as well: "Freud associates woman not only with the beginning of life but also with its end so that the figure of the mother fuses with that of death" (Sprengnether 1990: 5; cf. 153).

10. I concur with Kofman's view in this instance. However, I extend the argument beyond Kofman's, showing that Freud's complex and overdetermined compulsion to return to the animate/inanimate mechanical woman as a source of the uncanny is related to a rethinking of the trope of the "uncanny Jew" (a "living corpse," both "living and dead") (Shapiro 1997). See chapter 3.

11. An anticipation of these ideas on the "double" is present in a comment Freud made in a letter to Fliess after Fliess's pregnant wife and mother-in-law had been ill. "How uncanny," Freud wrote, "when mothers are shaky. They stand between us and [our] replacement." Quoted in Rizzuto (1998): 200, brackets in Rizzuto. "Our replacement," like the double, is closely associated with the uncanny, with mothers, and with death. Rizzuto shows that Masson (1985: 358) and others have mistranslated the passage (Rizzuto 1998: 199–200).

12. Joan Riviere's translation in the *Collected Papers* captures Freud's German better than Strachey's translation in the *Standard Edition* (*SE* 17: 244).

13. Lydenberg also notes this pattern: Freud's argument "brings him back twice to the uncanniness of the mother's body through the same textual sequence: a disquieting multiplicity of examples of the uncanny leads to a reference to the maternal body whereupon Freud ends the paragraph and inserts a break in the text" (1997: 1077).

14. See Rheingold for a discussion of clinical literature on the fantasy of death as a heavenly experience of reunion with the mother (1967: 12–13).

15. In "The Uncanny," the absence of God takes the shape of the presence of God's negative, the demons who replace the gods upon the collapse of religion: "The double has become a thing of terror, just as, after the collapse of their religion, the gods turned into demons" (*SE* 17: 236).

CHAPTER 3

1. Gilman states, for example, "Being Jewish is being male and being male is being Jewish . . . the Jewish male is the exemplary Jew for Freud" (1993: 199).

2. Cautioning against simplistic notions of "Jewishness" in this body of literature, Jay Geller points out the ambiguity of the term: "Is it a religious identity or an ethnic one — or following Rieff, a psychological one? Is it a tradition of interpretation, a certain hermeneutical practice or a predisposition? Is it an ethos that bears the signature of universal ethical monotheism? Is it an identity one chooses or an identity imposed? Is it a historical situation or a sociological fact?" (1997: 324). Like Geller, Le Rider inquires into the meanings of Jewishness, pointing out that Freud's discourse was one of Jewishness, *Jüdischkeit,* but not Judaism, *Judentum* (1993: 208).

3. Boyarin also draws attention to the relevance of postcolonial theory to an understanding of the Jews in post-emancipation Europe (1994). On the repres-

sion of the theme of homosexuality in Freud's understanding of Jewishness, see also Santner (1996), Geller (1997), and Eilberg-Schwartz (1994).

4. The theme of Freud's "ambivalence" about his Jewish identity is widely discussed. Chassaguet-Smirgel argues that ambivalence is inevitable for Jews in an anti-Semitic context: "To be a Jew of the Diaspora, living under the conditions that reigned at the end of the nineteenth and the first third of the twentieth century, and not to experience ambivalent feelings with regard to Judaism, would be purely and simply to escape the laws governing the human psyche" (1993: 84). Gilman (1986) interprets Freud's "ambivalence" as an expression of a malignant form of self-hatred *(Selbsthass);* Boyarin (1994) sees it as an analysis of (rather than an expression of) Jewish self-hatred in a post-colonial context; Le Rider argues that *Selbsthass* is not present in Freud's attitude toward his Jewish identity. Although I occasionally use the rather slippery term "ambivalence," I prefer to conceive of Freud's attitude neither as self-hatred, *Selbsthass,* nor as ambivalence, but as a series of attempts at analysis, some more successful than others. Boyarin's view is close to mine: "We have here not only an anatomy of misogyny and of antisemitism . . . but also of Jewish self-contempt" (1994: 37). See chapter 4 for a further discussion of these issues. In my view, as I suggested earlier, Freud was reformulating intellectually and analytically one of the central themes of *Kulturkritik* at the turn of the century: the "triangle of masculine, feminine and Jew" (Le Rider 1993: 171). In reaction against a century's dramatic progress in the emancipation of both women and Jews, this triangle took the negative form of a close intertwining of antifeminism and anti-Semitism. It took the positive form of creative (artistic and theoretical) renegotiations of Jewishness and gender that are particularly visible in Freud's work (Le Rider 1993: 183).

5. Psychoanalysts have sometimes interpreted overcoats in dreams as symbolic condoms. Freud's account of getting lost in the streets full of painted women, immediately followed by an account of death anxiety evoked by an overcoat, leads me to wonder whether he was expressing in condensed form a set of ideas associated not only with sexuality and death, but also with prostitution and venereal disease.

6. Klein (1985: 155–56) lists twenty-one addresses to the B'nai B'rith between 1897 and 1917, nine of them prior to 1903.

7. This translation is mine. The passage in Strachey's translation reads, "That you were Jews could only be agreeable to me, for I was myself a Jew and it had always seemed to me not only unworthy but positively senseless to deny

the fact. What bound me to Jewry was (I am ashamed to admit) neither faith nor national pride for I have always been an unbeliever and was brought up without any religion though not without a respect for what are called the 'ethical' standards of human civilization. . . . But plenty of other things remained over to make the attraction of Jewry and Jews irresistible [including] many obscure emotional forces which were the more powerful the less they could be expressed in words as well as a clear consciousness of an inner identity, the safe privacy of a common mental construction" (*SE* 20: 273–74).

8. Freud's sense of impending death was ongoing. For decades, he was known to take leave of his friends by saying, "Good-bye, you may never see me again" (Jones 1957: 301). By 1926, when he wrote the B'nai B'rith address, this awareness of his own mortality was particularly pressing. Although he would live another thirteen years, he knew that he was suffering from cancer.

9. Spero, too, finds feminine imagery in Freud's descriptions of his own Jewishness. He links Freud's Jewish identity with his frequent references "to innermost secrets, the uncanny, dark, irresistible forces, and in particular, the archaic heritage," noting that all of the "key metaphors (uncanny, obscure, mysterious forces) that play such an integral role in his analysis are feminine metaphors." Quoted in Ater (1992: x–xi), parentheses in the original.

10. Bakan argued that Kabbalah and psychoanalysis show striking similarities in "technique of interpretation and the importance and meaning attached to sexuality" (1958: 245). He proposed that "Freud, consciously or unconsciously, secularized Jewish mysticism" (25). Bakan's book concludes with a passage triumphantly integrating these threads: "Freud is then returning to the Mother who will provide him with forgiveness or acceptance in spite of the 'audacity' of his rebellion against the father-image. The sense of his oncoming death is the sense of punishment for his violation, and he permits himself, however so slightly, to accept the Mother's forgiveness in the form of immortality . . . he seeks comfort and safety in the Mother, the Holy Shekinah, the Community of Israel. That he, as Messiah, fought against the Father for the Mother's sake, makes him feel all the more that She will save him. And it is largely in this that the significance of *Heimlichkeit* lies" (1958: 317–18).

11. Bakan adds that Freud's theory of the uncanny was associated with an ambivalence about Judaism. He states, "we have in Freud's thought a complex which can be expressed as 'psychoanalysis-Jews-circumcision-uncanniness-rejection'" (1958: 307). Others draw similar conclusions. Ater notes that Freud "tried to understand it [the ambivalence] at least insofar as he observed it as a

part of himself. It was this contradictory feeling of attraction and repulsion, of intimacy and dread, that Freud stressed in his analysis of the 'holy,' the 'sacred' ... it was this, among other phenomena, that he had in mind in his study of the meaning of the German word *Heimlich*" (Ater 1992: 235).

12. I thank Jay Geller, who generously shared with me his thoughts and insights on the complex meanings of this anecdote in personal correspondence in 1998.

13. Again I thank Jay Geller for this insight.

14. Freud's son Martin recounts a memory which enacts an ironic reversal of Freud's attitude in this anecdote. On one occasion when Martin's young son was "behaving foolishly," Freud said "that there was not the slightest sense in becoming attached to a boy who must sooner or later kill himself in dangerous escapades" (Rizzuto 1998: 225).

15. The absence of a notion of immortality in the Torah, alongside the Gospel account of Jesus' encounter with the Sadducees on this issue, had led to a common assumption within both popular discourse and intellectual debate that Judaism lacks a doctrine of immortality.

16. Phillips notes that biographers emphasize that Freud was the "master of self-mastery," that "he chose his own death in the full light of its inevitability," and that "the death was of a piece with the life" (1999: 105–6). He warns, however, that biographers inevitably seek consistencies in the lives and deaths of their subjects and that biographies cannot contain the complexities of life and death.

CHAPTER 4

1. Freud was attentive to anti-Semitism in its diverse forms. See his remarks in "Resistances to Psychoanalysis" about anti-Semitism as a source of hostility to psychoanalysis: "The question may be raised whether the personality of the present writer as a Jew who has never sought to disguise the fact that he is a Jew may not have had a share in provoking the antipathy of his environment to psychoanalysis" (*SE* 19: 22).

2. These are not Freud's only published analyses of anti-Semitism. See, among many other references, *The Future of an Illusion* on the Aryan "illusion" of cultural superiority over other groups (*SE* 21), *Civilization and its Discontents* on the "narcissism of small differences" and the Jews' centuries of service as the

recipients or carriers of the projection of otherness for an anti-Jewish culture (*SE* 21), and "A Comment on Anti-Semitism" (*SE* 23: 287–293).

3. He reiterated this point a page later, emphasizing the disgust associated with women in the mind of the misogynist, but without using the term "uncanny": "Before the child comes under the dominance of the castration complex — at a time when he still holds woman at full value — he begins to display an intense desire to look . . . with the discovery that women do not have a penis, this longing often turns into its opposite and gives place to a feeling of disgust . . . impotence, misogyny, and permanent homosexuality" (*SE* 11: 96).

4. Cixous notes that the footnote is "a typographical metaphor of repression which is always too near, but nevertheless negligible" (1976: 537).

5. One might productively examine Freud's similar deferrals and evasions of gender and Jewishness in the Schreber case (*SE* 12: 1–80).

6. Kristeva reiterates her point: "The abomination provoked by the fertilizable or fertile feminine body (menses, childbirth)" is associated with impurity and defilement and are thus attributed to the mother and to women in general (1982: 100, parentheses in the original).

7. Kristeva is explicit about her universalism: "I have sought . . . to demonstrate on what mechanism of subjectivity (which I believe to be universal) such horror, its meaning as well as its power, is based" (1982: 208, parentheses in original). Is Freud a universalist in this regard? Clearly, as Boyarin notes, he "sets out to explain, almost to justify antisemitism" (Boyarin 1997: 241).

8. Kristeva's explicit and Freud's implicit interpretations of the intersections of anti-Semitism and misogyny are supported by the research of Elisabeth Young-Bruehl who, in *The Anatomy of Prejudices,* describes the typical prejudices of the obsessive and narcissistic characters. Young-Bruehl notes, on the one hand, the sexualization and feminization of the hated object, and, on the other, the rage against mastery and authority projected onto the hated object. The classic anti-Semite, she argues, is an obsessional character who "wants to eliminate a Jew who is both a filthy nothing and a secret, world-conquering conspirator" (1996: 239). To the narcissistic character, on the other hand, the Jew is either "effeminate or one of the chosen people of the cultural elite, that is, a person who can be construed as making a competitive claim to preeminence" (239). Young-Bruehl's obsessive and narcissistic anti-Semites therefore, articulate the two "deeper motives" named by Freud and Kristeva. What seems evident is that Freud's culture supported — and ours continues to support — a mix of obsessive and narcissistic prejudices in which hatred of the Jews and hatred of women are linked.

Young-Bruehl's analyses contribute to Freud's and Kristeva's attempts to uncover the sources and dynamics of this fear of the Other. Young-Bruehl also describes a third type, the hysteric, with no direct parallel in Kristeva's and Freud's analyses of xenophobia.

9. Lyotard develops a similar argument, suggesting that Freud's analysis of the terror aroused by sexual difference provides a way of articulating the terror aroused by the unrepresentable Other. The role of the Other, he states, is the role assigned to the Jews in Western European thought (Lyotard 1990: 19–23; cf. Le Rider 1993: 171). Although Lyotard focuses on the terror aroused by sexual difference, rather than fear of the maternal abject (Kristeva) or fear of the maternal genitals (Freud), his argument is close to both Freud's and Kristeva's. Lyotard states, "sexual difference . . . plays in the thought (in the psychic apparatus) of the (European) Occident this rule of an immanent terror. . . . 'The Jews' . . . are what cannot be domesticated in the obsession to dominate" (21–22, parentheses in the original). He goes on, "anti-Semitism is one of the means of the apparatus of its culture to bind and represent — to protect against — the originary terror" (23).

CHAPTER 5

1. *The Future of an Illusion* was begun in the spring of 1927, finished by September, and published in November 1927 (*SE* 21: 3); "Fetishism" was finished in August 1927 and published almost simultaneously (*SE* 21: 149).

2. See Homans (1989 and 1998) for a careful analysis of the symbolic loss engendered by the break with Jung and the role of Karl Abraham in the process of grieving that led to Freud's self-understanding, productivity, and creative work.

3. This is Phillips's translation.

4. Freud's question about why such truth and self-understanding is particularly accessible to the melancholic is reminiscent of the famous question posed to Oskar Pfister in 1918: "Why was it that none of all the pious ever discovered psychoanalysis? Why did it have to wait for a completely godless Jew?" (Meng and Freud 1963: 63). Freud's remarks in "Mourning and Melancholia" reflect a notion of the Jew as one with both a keener eye for truth and a melancholic disposition. "Mourning and Melancholia" thus hints obliquely at an association of the melancholic and the Jew. We shall see, however, that Jews take both the

position of the healthy mourner and the position of the melancholic in "On Transience."

5. Or perhaps the poet represents a fictionalized version of the poet Goethe?

6. "On Transience" can be productively read in relation to "On the History of the Psychoanalytic Movement," written just a few months earlier, in which Freud expresses rage and derision toward Jung, indicative of a temporary inability to mourn (Homans 1998: 77). By the time he wrote "On Transience," Freud had begun to come to terms with the loss of Jung as a member of the psychoanalytic movement.

7. Freud's interpretation of dreams of journeys as dreams of death (*SE* 5: 385) may be the appropriate hermeneutic here.

8. Santner, in an analysis of the "crisis of investiture" (by which he means disruptions in social roles and status) from which both the Nazi "Final Solution" and the paranoid and messianic fantasies of Judge Daniel Paul Schreber emerged (Schreber 1903), suggests that Freud's psychoanalytic theory represented an alternate reconstruction of this crisis. Freud was particularly sensitive to the crises and disruptions of modernity (1996: 17). Not unlike Homans, Santner sees fascism and psychoanalysis as opposite responses to the crises invoked by modernity.

9. The terror over the thought that his mother "might come to hear of [his] death" was shared by other members of Freud's family. According to a letter Freud wrote to his nephew Samuel in 1925, Amalie Freud could not tolerate hearing about any death in the family. Through a familial conspiracy of silence, she was protected from the knowledge of several deaths over many years: "We made a secret of all the losses in the family" (Clark 1980: 481).

10. Poor health prevented his attendance. His daughter Anna had become his emissary to many public events and ceremonies.

11. Donald Capps suggests that Carl Jung and Erik Erikson (along with psychologist William James and phenomenologist Rudolf Otto) experienced traumatic separations from their mothers which led to lifelong struggles with "melancholia" (Capps 1997). This melancholic disposition, in Capps's view, directed these men inexorably toward a psychological, introspective, and highly individualized encounter with religious ideas. Extending Capps's thesis, one might expect to find a similar relationship with the mother in Freud's case, since Freud clearly shared this psychological approach to religion with these four thinkers. Freud's response to his mother's death would seem to confirm

this application of Capps's thesis to Freud's case. Capps's provocative analysis might be expanded further into an analysis of cultural change in modernity. We might ask what sorts of social changes in the late nineteenth and early twentieth centuries influenced these men and these mothers and led to the emergence of these introspective individualized theories of religion.

12. In Sprengnether's view, Freud's difficulty acknowledging feelings of hostility toward the mother is not only an important element of his personal life, but also an important influence on the creation of the Oedipal theory: the Oedipal theory deflects rage toward the mother, redirecting it toward the father. She argues, "The Oedipal theory performs the function of acknowledging the anger . . . (murderous wishes directed toward the father) while enshrining an idealized memory of maternal love (mother-son incest)" (1995: 46, parentheses in the original). Other scholars, as well, have investigated the significance of Freud's relationship with his mother — and with the Catholic nursemaid or nanny employed by the Freud family during his first three years — for the later development of psychoanalytic theory. These scholars emphasize particular traumas in Freud's early childhood: the birth and death of a younger sibling, Julius, who lived only a few months, the close relationship with the nursemaid and her dismissal from the family's employment when Freud was less than three, and the family's move from Freiburg, Moravia (Pribor, Czechoslovakia) to Vienna in Freud's third year. In general, Freud's mother, Amalie, is described in this literature as narcissistically invested in her first-born child, her "Goldener Sigi." At the same time, she is seen as emotionally untrustworthy, and the loss of the nursemaid is seen as traumatic. As a result of his early experiences, these theorists argue, Freud's feelings toward his mother were fraught with conflict, anxiety, and fear of loss and abandonment which he was unable to express. These feelings were reflected, in turn, in the theories he constructed (Atwood and Stolorow 1993: 57–59; Roith 1987: 170; Sagan 1988; Margolis 1996; Sprengnether 1990, 1995; Rizzuto 1998). While these analyses of Freud's relationship with his mother and the origins of psychoanalytic theory are provocative, they ignore some important issues. First, while Sprengnether and others are correct that the Oedipal theory idealizes the mother-son relationship, we have seen that another picture of the mother emerges occasionally. We have traced in this volume the surfacing of the uncanny mother and the dead or deadly mother in Freud's texts. There is as much evidence for a non-Oedipal counterthesis as for the Oedipal masterplot

in these materials on Freud's earliest years. In addition, I am troubled by the pattern of blaming the mother, that is, the focus on the emotional untrustworthiness of Freud's mother as source of Freud's theory and character. It may be more productive to abandon the search for blameworthy episodes in Amalie's emotional makeup during the earliest years of Freud's life, to acknowledge that she did, in fact, raise a remarkable son, and to investigate the insights he developed into the cultural and psychological reproduction of misogyny. Rather than seeking pathology in his relationship with his mother or misogyny in his life and texts, we might examine instead Freud's ability, or inability, to experience maternal loss and his ability, or inability, to theorize it.

13. See Schiesari's complex analysis of the "gendering of melancholia" (1992). See also Sprengnether's analysis of the "open wound" of Emma Eckstein's botched surgery (1990: 22–38; 181–86).

EPILOGUE

1. The text reads: "If the Gates of Hell were a storefront on Main Street, wouldn't you tell the people going in about Jesus? . . . God uses sidewalk counselors in front of abortion clinics."

2. For a recent comedic film dealing with similar themes, see Mike Myers's *So I Married an Axe Murderer* (1993), which echoes Freud's "Three Caskets" in portraying the entanglement of desire for a beautiful woman with the fear of her deadly intentions. See also Bronfen's (1992) discussion of the fairy tale of Snow White, Hawthorne's tale "The Birthmark," and Sylvia Plath's *Bell Jar.* This pattern is also evident in the East. See Wilson's (1996) interpretation of the Tibetan Buddhist monastic practice of meditation upon a rotting female corpse, and Kakar's (1982) analysis of the fantasy of the mother's demonic eroticism in the Indian mythology of the horrific goddess Kali. The ideas and images of the counterthesis are not absent from Western religious discourse, either. The association of female sexuality and death emerges quite specifically in biblical texts. The book of Proverbs links Sheol, the realm of the dead, with seductive female sexuality, warning against the strange woman who seduces men: "Do not stray into her paths, for many a victim has she lain low; Yea, all her slain are a mighty host. Her house is the way to Sheol, going down to the chambers of death" (Prov. 7: 25–27; see also 30: 16 and Jon. 2: 3). In a psycho-

analytic interpretation of the Biblical book of Ezekiel, David Halperin suggests that "access to the dark and terrible realms . . . may be a necessary part of what religion means to us." But much of contemporary mainstream religion has turned away from the "dark and terrible realms." We encounter the dark and terrible elsewhere today.

    3. I thank Don Capps for drawing this text to my attention.

REFERENCES

Abraham, Hilda C., and Ernst L. Freud (1965). *A Psycho-Analytic Dialogue: The Letters of Sigmund Freud and Karl Abraham, 1907–1926,* trans. B. Marsh and H. C. Abraham. New York: Basic Books.

Alighieri, Dante (1961). *The Divine Comedy,* trans. and commentary by John Sinclair. New York: Oxford University Press.

Anzieu, Didier (1984). *The Group and the Unconscious.* London: Routledge.

———(1986). *Freud's Self-Analysis,* trans. Peter Graham. London: Hogarth.

Ater, Moshe (1992). *The Man Freud and Monotheism.* Jerusalem: The Magnes Press, The Hebrew University.

Atwood, George, and Robert Stolorow (1993). *Faces in a Cloud: Intersubjectivity in Personality Theory.* Northvale, New Jersey: Aronson.

Bakan, David (1958). *Sigmund Freud and the Jewish Mystical Tradition.* Boston: Beacon.

———(1966). *The Duality of Human Existence: Isolation and Communion in Western Man.* Boston: Beacon.

———(1967). *On Method: Toward a Reconstruction of Psychological Investigation.* San Francisco: Jossey-Bass.

Becker, Ernest (1973). *The Denial of Death.* New York: Macmillan.

Beers, William (1992). *Women and Sacrifice: Male Narcissism and the Psychology of Religion.* Detroit: Wayne State University Press.

——— (1995). "The Place of Mourning in Religion, History, and Theory." *Religious Studies Review* 21, 1: 9–13.

Benjamin, Jessica (1988). *The Bonds of Love: Psychoanalysis, Feminism, and the Problem of Domination.* New York: Pantheon Books.

Bettelheim, Bruno (1982). *Freud and Man's Soul.* New York: Knopf.

Bloom, Harold (1995). "Freud: Frontier Concepts, Jewishness, and Interpretation," in Cathy Caruth (ed.), *Trauma: Explorations in Memory,* 113–27. Baltimore: Johns Hopkins University Press.

Bonaparte, Marie, Anna Freud, and Ernst Kris (eds.) (1954). *The Origins of Psycho-Analysis: Letters to Wilhelm Fliess, Drafts and Notes, 1887–1902,* trans. Eric Mosbacher and James Strachey. New York: Basic Books. (*Aus den Anfängen der Psychoanalyse. Briefe an Wilhelm Fliess, Abhandlungen und Notizen aus den Jahren 1887–1902.* London: Imago, 1950.)

Boothby, Richard (1991). *Death and Desire: Psychoanalytic Theory in Lacan's Return to Freud.* New York: Routledge.

Boyarin, Daniel (1994). "Épater l'embourgeoisement: Freud, Gender, and the (De)Colonized Psyche." *Diacritics* 24: 17–41.

——— (1997). *Unheroic Conduct: The Rise of Heterosexuality and the Invention of the Jewish Man.* Berkeley: University of California Press.

Bregman, Lucy (1999). *Beyond Silence and Denial: Death and Dying Reconsidered.* Louisville: Westminster John Knox.

Brennan, Teresa (ed.) (1989). *Between Feminism and Psychoanalysis.* New York: Routledge.

Bronfen, Elizabeth (1992). *Over Her Dead Body.* London: Routledge.

Brooks, Peter (1989). "Freud's Masterplot," in David Richter (ed.), *The Critical Tradition: Classic Texts and Contemporary Trends,* 710–20. New York: St. Martin's Press.

Brown, Norman O. (1959). *Life Against Death: The Psychoanalytic Meaning of History.* Middletown, Connecticut: Wesleyan University Press.

Bruel, Karl (1953). *Cassell's German and English Dictionary.* London: Cassell and Company.

Buhle, Mari Jo (1998). *Feminism and its Discontents: A Century of Struggle with Psychoanalysis.* Cambridge: Harvard University Press.

Capps, Donald (1997). *Men, Religion, and Melancholia: James, Otto, Jung, and Erikson.* New Haven: Yale University Press.

Caruth, Cathy (1995). "An Interview with Robert Jay Lifton," in Cathy Caruth (ed.), *Trauma: Explorations in Memory,* 128–47. Baltimore: Johns Hopkins University Press.

Chanter, Tina (1995). *Ethics of Eros.* New York: Routledge.

Chassaguet-Smirgel, Jannine (1993). "Some Thoughts on Freud's Attitude during the Nazi Period," in David Meghnagi (ed.), *Freud and Judaism,* trans. Mark Solms, 73–92. London: Karnac Books.

Chodorow, Nancy (1978). *The Reproduction of Mothering: Psychoanalysis and the Sociology of Gender.* Berkeley: University of California Press.

———(1989). *Feminism and Psychoanalytic Theory.* New Haven: Yale University Press.

Chopp, Rebecca (1993). "From Patriarchy into Freedom: A Conversation Between American Feminist Theology and French Feminism," in C. W. Maggie Kim, Susan M. St. Ville, and Susan M. Simonaitis (eds.), *Transfigurations: Theology and the French Feminists,* 31–48. Minneapolis: Fortress.

Cixous, Hélène (1981). "The Laugh of the Medusa," in Elaine Marks and Isabelle de Courtivron (eds.), *New French Feminisms.* New York: Schocken Books.

———(1976). "Fiction and Its Phantoms: A Reading of Freud's *'Das Unheimliche'* ('The Uncanny')." *New Literary History 7,* 3: 525–48.

Clark, R. W. (1980). *Freud, The Man and the Cause: A Biography.* New York: Random House.

Clark, William R. (1996). *Sex and the Origins of Death.* New York: Oxford University Press.

Cuddihy, John Murray (1987). *The Ordeal of Civility.* Boston: Beacon.

Deleuze, Gilles, and Félix Guattari (1983). *Anti-Oedipus: Capitalism and Schizophrenia,* trans. Robert Hurley, Mark Seem, and Helen Lane. Minneapolis: University of Minnesota Press.

Derrida, Jacques (1995). *Archive Fever.* Chicago: University of Chicago Press.

———(1998). *Resistances of Psychoanalysis,* trans. Peggy Kamuf, Pascale-Anne Brault, and Michael Naas. Stanford: Stanford University Press.

DiCenso, James (1999). *The Other Freud.* New York: Routledge.

Diller, Jerry (1991). *Freud's Jewish Identity.* Rutherford, N.J.: Farleigh Dickinson University Press.

Dollinger, Phillipe (1970). *The German Hansa,* trans. and ed. D. S. Ault and S. H. Steinberg. Stanford: Stanford University Press.

Eilberg-Schwartz, Howard (1990). *The Savage in Judaism.* Bloomington: Indiana University Press.

———— (1994). *God's Phallus and Other Problems for Men and Monotheism.* Boston: Beacon.

Erikson, Erik (1964). *Insight and Responsibility: Lectures on the Ethical Implications of Psychoanalytic Insight.* New York: Norton.

Feldman, Yael (1994). "'And Rebecca Loved Jacob,' but Freud Did Not," in Peter Rudnytsky and Ellen Handler Spitz (eds.), *Freud and Forbidden Knowledge,* 7–25. New York: New York University Press.

Feldstein, Richard, and Judith Roof (eds.) (1989). *Feminism and Psychoanalysis.* Ithaca: Cornell University Press.

Felski, Rita (1995). *The Gender of Modernity.* Cambridge: Harvard University Press.

Flax, Jane (1990). *Thinking Fragments: Psychoanalysis, Feminism, and Postmodernism in the Contemporary West.* Berkeley: University of California Press.

Foucault, Michel (1980 [1978]). *The History of Sexuality, Volume 1: An Introduction,* trans. Robert Hurley. New York: Vintage.

Freeman, Lucy, and Herbert Strean (1987). *Freud and Women.* New York: Continuum.

Freud, Ernst, and Lucie Freud (eds.) (1960). *Sigmund Freud Briefe: 1873–1938.* Frankfurt am Main: S. Fischer Verlag.

Freud, Ernst (ed.) (1992). *Letters of Sigmund Freud, 1873–1939,* trans. Tania Stern and James Stern. New York: Dover.

———— (ed.) (1970). *The Letters of Sigmund Freud and Arnold Zweig,* trans. Elaine Robson-Scott and William Robson-Scott. New York: Harcourt, Brace and World.

Freud, Sigmund (1924–1928). *Gesammelte Schriften (GS).* Vienna: Internationaler Psychoanalytischer Verlag.

———— (1928). *Die Zukunft einer Illusion. GS* 11: 411–66.

———— (1928). "Ein religiöses Erlebnis." *GS* 11: 467–70.

———— (1942). *Gesammelte Werke (GW).* Volumes 2 and 3. Frankfurt am Main: S. Fischer Verlag.

———— (1946). *Collected Papers (CP).* Volume 4, trans. and ed. Joan Riviere. London: Hogarth Press.

———— (1953–1974). *The Standard Edition of the Complete Psychological Works of Sigmund Freud (SE).* Volumes 1–24, trans. and ed. James Strachey. London: Hogarth Press.

——— (1961). "Address Delivered in the Goethe House at Frankfurt." *SE* 21: 207–74.

——— (1959). "Address to the Society of B'nai B'rith." *SE* 20: 273.

——— (1955). "Analysis of a Phobia in a Five-Year-Old Boy." *SE* 10: 5–153.

——— (1955). "Beyond the Pleasure Principle." *SE* 18: 3–143.

——— (1961). *Civilization and its Discontents. SE* 21: 64–148.

——— (1964). "A Comment on Anti-Semitism." *SE* 23: 287–93.

——— (1961). "Dissolution of the Oedipus Complex." *SE* 19: 172–79.

——— (1961). "Dostoevksy and Parricide." *SE* 21: 175–97.

——— (1961). "Economic Problem of Masochism." *SE* 19: 157–70.

——— (1961). "Ego and the Id." *SE* 19: 3–66.

——— (1955). "Extracts from the Fliess Papers." *SE* 1: 175–282.

——— (1961). "Female Sexuality." *SE* 21: 223–45.

——— (1961). "Fetishism." *SE* 21: 151–57.

——— (1961). *The Future of an Illusion. SE* 21: 5–58.

——— (1957). "On the History of the Psychoanalytic Movement." *SE* 14: 3–66.

——— (1961). "On Humor." *SE* 21: 159–66.

——— (1961). "Infantile Genital Organization." *SE* 19: 139–45.

——— (1959). "Inhibitions, Symptoms and Anxiety." *SE* 20: 77–174.

——— (1953). *The Interpretation of Dreams. SE* 4–5: 1–722.

——— (1963). *Introductory Lectures on Psychoanalysis. SE* 15: 1–239.

——— (1955). "Leonardo Da Vinci and a Memory of His Childhood." *SE* 11: 59–138.

——— (1955). "Letter 71" (Extracts from the Fliess Papers). *SE* 1: 175–282.

——— (1955). "The Medusa's Head." *SE* 18: 273–74.

——— (1964). *Moses and Monotheism. SE* 23: 1–138.

——— (1957). "Mourning and Melancholia." *SE* 14: 239–57.

——— (1961). "On Negation." *SE* 19: 235–40.

——— (1964). *New Introductory Lectures. SE* 22: 3–183.

——— (1961). "Note upon the Mystic Writing Pad." *SE* 19: 227–32.

——— (1958). "Occurrence in Dreams of Material from Fairy Tales." *SE* 12: 281–87.

——— (1958). "Psychoanalytic Notes on an Autobiographical Account of a Case of Paranoia." *SE* 12: 1–80.

——— (1961). "A Religious Experience." *SE* 21: 167–72.

——— (1958). "Remembering, Repeating, and Working Through." *SE* 12: 145–56.

————(1961). "Resistances to Psychoanalysis." *SE* 19: 213–22.

————(1961). "Some Psychical Consequences of the Anatomical Distinction between the Sexes." *SE* 19: 243–58.

————(1957). "A Special Type of Choice of Object Made by Men." *SE* 11: 163–76.

————(1957). "Taboo of Virginity." *SE* 11: 193–207.

————(1958). "Theme of the Three Caskets." *SE* 12: 291–301.

————(1957). "Thoughts for the Times on War and Death." *SE* 14: 275–301.

————(1953). "Three Essays on Sexuality." *SE* 7: 125–248.

————(1955). *Totem and Taboo. SE* 13: 1–163.

————(1957). "On Transience." *SE* 14: 303–7.

————(1955). "Two Encyclopedia Articles." *SE* 18: 235–59.

————(1955). "The Uncanny." *SE* 17: 217–56.

————(1957). "The Unconscious (Papers on Metapsychology)." *SE* 14: 159–206.

————(1993). "Death and Us," in David Meghnagi (ed.), *Freud and Judaism,* trans. Mark Solms. London: Karnac Books ([1915] "Wir und der Tod," Zweimonats-Bericht für die Mitglieder der Osterr. Israel Humanitätsvereine 'B'nai B'rith,' 18, no. 1, 1915: 41–51).

Friedan, Betty (1963). *The Feminine Mystique.* New York: Norton.

Frieden, Ken (1990). *Freud's Dream of Interpretation.* Albany: State University of New York Press.

Friedlander, Stephen (1996). "Field Notes: Conference on Spirituality and Psychoanalysis." *Journal of Psychoanalysis, Culture, and Society* 1, 2: 170–73.

Garner, Shirley (1985). "Introduction," in Shirley Garner, Claire Kahane, and Madelon Sprengnether (eds.), *The (M)other Tongue: Essays in Feminist Psychoanalytic Interpretation,* 15–29. Ithaca: Cornell University Press.

Gay, Peter (1987). *A Godless Jew: Freud, Atheism, and the Meaning of Psychoanalysis.* New Haven: Yale.

————(1988). *Freud: A Life for Our Time.* New York: Norton.

————(1999). "Psychoanalyst Sigmund Freud (Great Minds of the Century)." *Time,* 153, 12: 64–69 (March 29, 1999).

Geller, Jay (1992a). "A Glance at the Nose: Freud's Inscription of Jewish Difference." *American Imago* 49: 427–44.

————(1992b). "(G)nos(e)ology: The Cultural Construction of the Other," in Howard Eilberg-Schwartz (ed.), *People of the Body: Jews and Judaism from* an *Embodied Perspective,* 243–82. Albany: State University of New York Press.

—— (1993). "A Paleontological View of Freud's Study of Religion: Unearthing the *Leitfossil* Circumcision." *Modern Judaism* 13: 49–70.

——(1997). "Identifying 'Someone Who Is Himself One of Them': Recent Studies of Freud's Jewish Identity." *Religious Studies Review* 23: 323–31.

—— (1999). "The Godfather of Psychoanalysis: Circumcision, Anti-semitism, Homosexuality, and Freud's 'Fighting Jew,'" *Journal of the American Academy of Religion* 67, 2: 355–86.

Gilligan, Carol (1984). "Conquistadors of the Dark Continent." *Daedalus* 3, 75–95.

Gilman, Sander (1986). *Jewish Self-Hatred: Anti-Semitism and the Hidden Language of the Jews.* Baltimore: Johns Hopkins.

——(1993). *Freud, Race, and Gender.* Princeton: Princeton University Press.

Gold, Michael (1985). *A Conspiracy of Cells: One Woman's Immortal Legacy and the Medical Scandal it Caused.* Albany: State University of New York Press.

Goldenberg, Naomi (1990). *Returning Words to Flesh: Feminism, Psychoanalysis, and the Resurrection of the Body.* Boston: Beacon.

——(1997). "A Theory of Gender as a Central Hermeneutic in the Psychoanalysis of Religion," in Jacob Belzen (ed.), *Hermeneutical Approaches in the Psychology of Religion,* 65–84. Amsterdam and Atlanta: Editions Rodopi.

Graf, Max (1942). "Reminiscences of Professor Sigmund Freud." *Psychoanalytic Quarterly* 11: 465–76.

Greer, Germaine (1971). *The Female Eunuch.* New York: McGraw-Hill.

Gresser, Moshe (1994). *Dual Allegiance: Freud as a Modern Jew.* Albany: State University of New York Press.

Grinstein, Alexander (1968). *On Sigmund Freud's Dreams.* Detroit: Wayne State University Press.

Grubrich-Simitis, Ilse (1996). *Back to Freud's Texts: Making Silent Documents Speak,* trans. Philip Slotkin. New Haven: Yale University Press.

Grunberger, Bela (1988). "The Oedipal Conflicts of the Analyst," trans. Marion M. Oliner, in George H. Pollock and John Munder Ross (eds.), *The Oedipus Papers,* 261–83. New York: International Universities Press.

Halperin, David (1993). *Seeking Ezekiel: Text and Psychology.* State College: Pennsylvania State University Press.

Handelman, Susan (1982). *The Slayers of Moses: The Emergence of Rabbinic*

Interpretation in Modern Literary Theory. Albany: State University of New York Press.

Homans, Peter (1970). *Theology after Freud.* Indianapolis: Bobbs-Merrill.

—— (1989). *The Ability to Mourn: Disillusionment and the Social Origins of Psychoanalysis.* Chicago: University of Chicago Press.

—— (1995 [1979]). *Jung In Context.* Second edition. Chicago: University of Chicago Press.

—— (1998). "We (Not-So) Happy Few: Symbolic Loss and Mourning in Freud's Psychoanalytic Movement and the History of Psychoanalysis." *Psychoanalysis and History* 1: 69–86.

Hyman, Stanley Edgar (1962). *The Tangled Bank.* New York: Atheneum.

Jacobs, Janet (1997). "Freud as Other: Anti-Semitism and the Development of Psychoanalysis," in Janet Liebman Jacobs and Donald Capps (eds.), *Religion, Society, and Psychoanalysis: Readings in Contemporary Theory,* 28–41. Boulder: Westview.

Jay, Nancy (1992). *Throughout Your Generations Forever: Sacrifice, Religion, and Paternity.* Chicago: University of Chicago Press.

Jones, Ernest (1953). *Sigmund Freud, Life and Work: Volume One.* London: Hogarth.

—— (1955). *Sigmund Freud, Life and Work: Volume Two.* London: Hogarth.

—— (1957). *Sigmund Freud, Life and Work: Volume Three.* London: Hogarth.

Jones, James (1996). *Religion and Psychology in Transition: Psychoanalysis, Feminism, and Theology.* New Haven: Yale University Press.

Jonte-Pace, Diane (1987). "Object Relations Theory, Mothering, and Religion: Toward a Feminist Psychology of Religion." *Horizons* 14, 2: 310–27.

—— (1992). "Situating Kristeva Differently," in David Crownfield (ed.), *Body/Text in Julia Kristeva: Religion, Women, and Psychoanalysis,* 1–22. Albany: State University of New York Press.

—— (1993). "Psychoanalysis after Feminism." *Religious Studies Review* 19, 2: 110–15.

—— (1996). "At Home in the Uncanny: Freudian Representations of Death, Mothers, and the Afterlife." *Journal of the American Academy of Religion* 64: 61–88.

—— (1997a). "Julia Kristeva and the Psychoanalytic Study of Religion: Rethinking Freud's Cultural Texts," in Janet Liebman Jacobs and Donald Capps (eds.), *Religion, Society, and Psychoanalysis: Readings in Contemporary Theory,* 240–68. Boulder: Westview.

———(1997b). "New Directions in Feminist Psychology of Religion." *Journal of Feminist Studies in Religion* 13: 63–74.

——— (1999a). "In Defense of an Unfriendly Freud: Psychoanalysis, Feminism, and Theology." *Pastoral Psychology* 47, 3: 175–82.

———(1999b). "'Legitimation of Hatred or Inversion into Love': Religion in Kristeva's Re-Reading of Freud." *Journal of Research in the Social Scientific Study of Religion* 10: 17–35.

———(2001). "Analysts, Critics, and Inclusivists: Feminist Voices in the Psychology of Religion," in Diane Jonte-Pace and William Parsons (eds.), *Religion and Psychology: Mapping the Terrain,* 129–46. London: Routledge.

Jung, Carl (1963). *Memories, Dreams, Reflections.* New York: Vintage.

Kakar, Sudhir (1982). *Shamans, Mystics and Doctors: A Psychological Inquiry into India and its Healing Traditions.* Boston: Beacon.

Kearns, Cleo (1993). "Kristeva and Feminist Theology," in C. W. Maggie Kim, Susan M. St. Ville and Susan M. Simonaitis (eds.), *Transfigurations: Theology and the French Feminists,* 49–80. Minneapolis: Fortress Press.

Klein, Dennis (1985). *Jewish Origins of the Psychoanalytic Movement.* Chicago: University of Chicago Press.

Klein, Melanie (1975). *Love, Guilt and Reparation and Other Works, 1921–1945,* trans. and ed. R. E. Money-Kyrle et al. London: Hogarth.

Kofman, Sarah (1985). *The Enigma of Woman: Woman in Freud's Writings,* trans. Catherine Porter. Ithaca: Cornell University Press.

——— (1991). *Freud and Fiction,* trans. Sarah Wykes. Boston: Northeastern University Press.

Kohut, Heinz (1971). *The Analysis of the Self: A Systematic Approach to the Psychoanalytic Treatment of Narcissistic Personality Disorders.* New York: International Universities Press.

Kristeva, Julia (1982). *Powers of Horror: An Essay on Abjection,* trans. Leon Roudiez. New York: Columbia University Press.

——— (1987). *In the Beginning Was Love: Psychoanalysis and Faith,* trans. Arthur Goldhammer. New York: Columbia University Press.

——— (1989). *Black Sun: Depression and Melancholia,* trans. Leon Roudiez. New York: Columbia University Press.

———(1991). *Strangers to Ourselves,* trans. Leon Roudiez. New York: Columbia University Press.

Küng, Hans (1990). *Freud and the Problem of God.* New Haven: Yale University Press.

Lacan, Jacques (1977). *Écrits: A Selection,* trans. Alan Sheridan. New York: Norton.

LaPlanche, Jean (1976). *Life and Death in Psychoanalysis,* trans. Jeffrey Mehlman. Baltimore: Johns Hopkins University Press.

Le Rider, Jacques (1993). *Modernity and Crises of Identity: Culture and Society in Fin de Siècle Vienna,* trans. Rosemary Morris. New York: Continuum.

Lutzky, Harriet (1991). "The Sacred and the Maternal Object: An Application of Fairbairn's Theory to Religion," in H. Siegal et al. (eds.), *Psychoanalytic Reflections on Current Issues,* 25–44. New York: New York University Press.

Lydenberg, Robin (1997). "Freud's Uncanny Narratives." *Publications of the Modern Language Association of America* 112, 5: 1072–86.

Lyotard, Jean-François (1990). *Heidegger and "the jews,"* trans. Andreas Michel and Mark Roberts. Minneapolis: University of Minnesota Press.

Margolis, Deborah (1996). *Freud and His Mother: Preoedipal Aspects of Freud's Personality.* Northvale, N.J.: Jason Aaronson.

Masson, Jeffrey (trans. and ed.) (1985) *The Complete Letters of Sigmund Freud to Wilhelm Fliess, 1887–1904.* Cambridge: Harvard University Press.

McGrath, William (1986). *Freud's Discovery of Psychoanalysis: The Politics of Hysteria.* Ithaca: Cornell University Press.

McGuire, William (ed.) (1974). *The Freud/Jung Letters: The Correspondence between Sigmund Freud and C. G. Jung,* trans. Ralph Manheim and R. F. C. Hull. Princeton: Princeton University Press.

Meghnagi, David (ed.) (1993). *Freud and Judaism,* trans. Mark Solms. London: Karnac Books.

Meissner, William (1984) *Psychoanalysis and Religion.* New Haven: Yale University Press.

Meng, Heinrich, and Ernst Freud (eds.) (1963). *Psychoanalysis and Faith: The Letters of Sigmund Freud and Oskar Pfister,* trans. Eric Mosbacher. New York: Basic Books.

Merkur, Daniel (1997). "Freud and Hasidim," in Janet Liebman Jacobs and Donald Capps (eds.), *Religion, Society, and Psychoanalysis: Readings in Contemporary Theory,* 11–22. Boulder: Westview.

Miller, Justin (1981). "Interpretations of Freud's Jewishness, 1924–1974." *Journal of the History of the Behavioral Sciences* 17, 3: 357–74.

Millet, Kate (1970). *Sexual Politics.* Garden City, N.Y.: Doubleday.

Mitchell, Juliet (1974). *Psychoanalysis and Feminism: Freud, Reich, Laing, and Women.* New York: Random House.

Mitscherlich, Margarete (1985). *Die Friedfertige Frau: Ein Psychoanalytische Untersuchung zur Aggression der Geschlechter.* Frankfurt am Main: S. Fischer Verlag.

Oring, Elliott (1984). *The Jokes of Sigmund Freud.* Philadelphia: University of Pennsylvania Press.

Parsons, William (1999). *The Enigma of the Oceanic Feeling.* New York: Oxford University Press.

Paul, Robert (1991). "Freud's Anthropology: A Reading of the 'Cultural Books,'" in Jerome Neu (ed.), *The Cambridge Companion to Freud,* 267–86. New York: Cambridge University Press.

Phillips, Adam (1999). *Darwin's Worms.* New York: Basic Books.

Pollock, George, and John Ross (1988). "Introduction" in *The Oedipus Papers,* George Pollock and John Ross (eds.). Monograph 6, Classics in Psychoanalysis, xv–xix. Madison, Conn.: International Universities Press.

Pontalis, Jean Baptiste (1978). "On Death-Work in Freud, in the Self, in Culture," in Alan Roland (ed.), *Psychoanalysis, Creativity, and Literature,* trans. Susan Cohen, 85–95. New York: Columbia University Press.

Raab, Kelley (1997). "Nancy Jay and a Feminist Psychology of Sacrifice." *Journal of Feminist Studies in Religion,* 13: 75–89.

Rand, Nicholas, and Maria Torok (1997). *Questions for Freud: The Secret History of Psychoanalysis.* Cambridge: Harvard University Press.

Rheingold, Joseph (1967). *The Mother, Anxiety, and Death: The Catastrophic Death Complex.* Boston: Little, Brown and Co.

Rice, Emmanuel (1990). *Freud and Moses: The Long Journey Home.* Albany: State University of New York Press.

Ricoeur, Paul (1970). *Freud and Philosophy.* New Haven: Yale University Press.

Rieff, Philip (1966). *Triumph of the Therapeutic.* New York: Harpers.

——— (1979). *Freud: The Mind of the Moralist.* Chicago: University of Chicago Press.

Rizzuto, Ana Maria (1979). *The Birth of the Living God: A Psychoanalytic Study.* Chicago: University of Chicago Press.

——— (1998). *Why Did Freud Reject God? A Psychodynamic Interpretation.* New Haven: Yale University Press.

Robert, Marthe (1976). *From Oedipus to Moses: Freud's Jewish Identity,* trans. R. Manheim. Garden City, N.Y.: Doubleday.

Rohde-Dachser, Christa (1991). *Expedition in den dunklen Kontinent: Weiblichkeit im Diskurs der Psychoanalyse.* Berlin: Springer Verlag.

Roith, Estelle (1987). *The Riddle of Freud: Jewish Influences on his Theory of Female Sexuality*. London: Tavistock.

Ross, Mary Ellen, and Cheryl Lynn Ross (1983). "Mothers, Infants, and the Psychoanalytic Study of Ritual." *Signs: Journal of Women in Culture and Society* 9, 1: 27–39.

Rudnytsky, Peter (1987). *Freud and Oedipus*. New York: Columbia University Press.

Sagan, Eli (1988). *Freud, Women, and Morality*. New York: Basic Books.

Santner, Eric (1996). *My Own Private Germany: Daniel Paul Schreber's Secret History of Modernity*. Princeton: Princeton University Press.

Schiesari, Juliana (1992). *The Gendering of Melancholia: Feminism, Psychoanalysis, and the Symbolics of Loss in Renaissance Literature*. Ithaca: Cornell University Press.

Schorske, Carl (1973). "Politics and Patricide in Freud's Interpretation of Dreams." *American Historical Review* 78: 328–47.

Schreber, Daniel Paul (2000 [1903]). *Memoirs of My Nervous Illness*. New York Review of Books Press.

Schur, Max (1972). *Freud: Living and Dying*. New York: International Universities Press.

Shapiro, Susan (1997). "The Uncanny Jew: A Brief History of an Image." *Judaism* 46, 1: 63–78.

Shengold, Leonard (1991). *"Father, Don't You See I'm Burning?" Reflections on Sex, Narcissism, Symbolism, and Murder: From Everything to Nothing*. New Haven: Yale University Press.

Simon, Bennett, and Rachel Blass (1991). "The Development and Vicissitudes of Freud's Ideas on the Oedipus Complex," in Jerome Neu (ed.), *The Cambridge Companion to Freud*, 161–74. New York: Cambridge University Press.

Sprengnether, Madelon (1990). *The Spectral Mother: Freud, Feminism, and Psychoanalysis*. Ithaca: Cornell University Press.

——— (1995). "Reading Freud's Life." *American Imago* 52, 1: 9–54.

Sulloway, Frank (1979). *Freud, Biologist of the Mind: Beyond the Psychoanalytic Legend*. New York: Basic Books.

Todd, Marie Hane (1986). "The Veiled Woman in Freud's 'Das Unheimliche.'" *Signs: Journal of Women in Culture and Society* 11, 3: 519–28.

Toews, John (1991). "Historicizing Psychoanalysis: Freud in His Time and for Our Time." *Journal of Modern History* 63: 504–45.

Torgovnick, Marianna (1990). *Gone Primitive: Savage Intellects, Modern Lives.* Chicago: University of Chicago Press.

Van Herik, Judith (1982). *Freud on Femininity and Faith.* Berkeley: University of California Press.

Viereck, George (1930). *Glimpses of the Great.* London: Duckworth.

Wallwork, Ernest (1991). *Psychoanalysis and Ethics.* New Haven: Yale University Press.

Walter, Tony (1996). *The Eclipse of Eternity: A Sociology of the Afterlife.* New York: St. Martin's Press.

Wasserstrom, Steven (1999). *Religion after Religion.* Princeton, N.J.: Princeton University Press.

Weiner, Marc (1995). *Richard Wagner and the Anti-Semitic Imagination.* Lincoln: University of Nebraska Press.

Wilson, Liz (1996). *Charming Cadavers: Horrific Figurations of the Feminine in Indian Buddhist Hagiographic Literature.* Chicago: University of Chicago Press.

Winnicott, Donald W. (1972). *Playing and Reality.* London: Tavistock Publications.

Wittels, Fritz (1924). *Sigmund Freud: His Personality, His Teaching, and His School,* trans. T. Eden and C. Paul. London: Allen and Unwin.

Wittgenstein, Ludwig (1966). *Lectures and Conversations in Aesthetics, Psychology, and Religious Belief.* Berkeley: University of California Press.

Wulff, David M. (1997). *Psychology of Religion: Classic and Contemporary Views.* Second edition. New York: Wiley.

www.ihatewomen.com.

www.operationrescue.com

www.prochoice.about.com

Yerushalmi, Yosef Hayim (1991). *Freud's Moses: Judaism Terminable and Interminable.* New Haven: Yale University Press.

Young-Bruehl, Elisabeth (1996). *The Anatomy of Prejudices.* Cambridge: Harvard University Press.

INDEX

Compositor:	BookMatters, Berkeley
Text:	10/15 Granjon
Display:	Granjon
Printer and Binder:	Haddon Craftsmen, Inc.